CONTENTS

PREFACE

MY STORY: A ROLLER COASTER
OF EMOTIONS

When I was ten years old, I was in a roller coaster accident that
changed the course of my life. Although I was barely tall enough
to reach the minimum allowable height on the measuring tape
that afternoon, I was excited beyond words for my first roller
coaster experience. Over the years, my two older sisters had
enjoyed this thrill—while I watched from a distance. Not this
time! I received the nod of approval and began to eagerly
climb the stairs, my sisters and dad in tow.

I was a naturally adventurous and curious child. There was
nothing I loved more than a challenge—and what could be
more challenging than a scary roller coaster ride? Once seated
and buckled in, despite my brave face, I found myself terrified.
This fear felt different from other fears that I had experienced
before—made more intense by the fact that I couldn't change
my mind. Fortunately, my older sister was in the seat behind me:
her presence made me feel a little more safe and calm.

The ride started off slowly, with the rhythmic sounds of the
cart moving over tracks. We quickly picked up speed as we entered
the first corner. I closed my eyes tight and repeated to myself,
"This is fun"—even though deep down it didn't feel that way.

After we'd swept around that first corner, I tentatively opened my eyes and turned to glimpse my dad and other sister in the cart behind. Then our cart jerked around another corner and accelerated down a dip. When I turned to face forwards again, I saw that the cart ahead of us had come to a stop. However, ours didn't seem to be slowing down. It kept gaining speed. Next thing, we slammed directly into the cart in front. Upon impact, my body was involuntarily propelled forwards, causing the seat-belt to dig painfully into my chest.

Our cart immediately began to reverse quite rapidly for a few seconds (there was a big gap between us and Dad's cart), then proceeded to hurtle forwards once more. Everything happened so fast that I thought it was all planned—part of the ride. It was as if the ride had morphed into a kind of dodgem and our cart had done a run-up ready to dislodge the cart in front. We rammed into it again and this time came to a complete halt.

Upon the second impact, time stood still, as though I'd entered a dream. In this dream I was safe and nothing in the world was wrong. Faintly, I could hear howls of pain but they were a long way off. If I stayed perfectly still, then hopefully whatever scary thing was causing those howls couldn't touch me.

"Are you okay?"—it was Dad's voice; he had climbed out from the cart behind us and made his way down the roller coaster tracks. The moment his face appeared in front of me, my bubble burst open. The quiet, distant sounds in my dream suddenly changed to roaring in my ears, and with that came the terrifying realization that I could barely breathe.

Terror gripped me. Every fiber of my being screamed to get out of there. Frantically, I tried to wriggle myself free, but my seatbelt was so tight across my chest that I couldn't move at all. I was trapped.

Over the course of the next several hours I dipped in and out of my dream-like state. Whenever I became lucid, all around there was a hum of activity. I would find myself watching helicopters fly over, scaffolding being erected; paramedics appeared, placed an oxygen mask on my face and then disappeared. Eventually, my sister and I were extracted from the cart, strapped into stretchers and carried back down to solid ground.

Some days later, it was explained to me that it was a mechanical malfunction that had caused the cart ahead of us to stop. A number of people were taken to hospital but were discharged the same day. My sister and I had sustained the worst injuries. It would be a month before I returned home.

My injuries were primarily internal: a lacerated spleen, dislocated shoulder and—the most serious of all—my heart had been damaged. It had been bruised (myocardial contusion) by the impact. At first, the main concern was the potential of heart attack. Thankfully that didn't happen, but my heart rate was—and remains—in a seriously elevated state.

After I was moved from Emergency and on to the ward, my family brought me a bag of my clothes and my most comforting and beloved possession—my red Teletubby, Po. I always had it by my side at night in bed. During the month I was in hospital I had to undergo daily tests. There was also a surgical procedure to check whether or not there was a blockage in one of the arteries of my heart. Although Po accompanied me into the operating theater, she didn't make it out: no one could find her. This was a devastating blow to me, and one I didn't let go of until long after my discharge from hospital.

Each day in hospital dragged: for a ten-year-old, a month feels like an eternity. But being allowed to go home was bitter-sweet as I had to take a heart monitor with me. I felt terribly self-conscious wearing it under my school clothes. The wires weren't easily disguised. Also, for the next eight years I had frequent hospital appointments and physical tests.

Nowadays, when I focus on the accident my recollections are both incredibly vivid and, at the same time, incredibly vague. I can visualize certain moments, but then it's like an eraser has been rubbed over the next part of the story, creating a disjointed and confusing timeline.

That feeling of confusion, of not having continuity and resolution, was ultimately what scared me the most, especially as a ten-year-old. It buried itself deep into my bones, so that every day I would carry the weight of feeling that I no longer made sense and that any control I'd had over myself and the world around me had been shattered. Once those feelings arrived, they made themselves at home without consent.

My mind was in total opposition, however, pretending and maintaining that there was absolutely nothing wrong, the experience hadn't impacted me and that I didn't need any sort of "special" treatment. There was a constant battle being waged inside of me: my body versus my mind.

Slowly, a numbness crept through me and took over, dimming the physical, emotional and psychological pain of the whole experience and creating a steely exterior that protected me from myself as well as from the inquiries and expressions of concern from those around me. This protective bubble was impenetrable for the most part; it was only during sleep that I was unable to maintain my guard. Over and over again I would wake gasping for air, visited by overwhelming feelings of being trapped and wanting to get up and run away from the whole experience.

As time passed, my sense of helplessness and frustration grew. I viewed myself as strong, so why did I keep feeling pain or thinking dark thoughts? Things I considered that weak people did. The list of frustrations was never-ending and it included: the frequent hospital appointments, having to wear medical devices that didn't fit in the pockets of my school trousers and having to answer questions about my state. At first, the frustration was directed at myself, but eventually it spilled over to being agitated and annoyed at everyone else—why were they making a big deal out of this? Why wouldn't they treat me normally?

The after-effects of my physical injuries annoyed me too. Thanks to the permanent damage my heart had sustained, it was a struggle to keep up with any increase in energy expenditure. Even simple things like coughing or sneezing would raise my heart rate to over 200 beats per minute (a healthy heart rate for a 10-year-old is 60–100). Tiredness shadowed me: I couldn't make it through a whole day of school, I couldn't play sports and I couldn't be the energetic kid I'd been before the accident.

It wasn't long before I was fed up with being "the kid who'd been in a roller coaster accident" and felt trapped by the person

I'd become. What I wanted to do was reach back into the past to revive the former version of me, but I didn't know where to even start. On that day back in spring, I'd gone from being energetic, outgoing and adventurous to exhausted, sullen and hyper-reactive.

The term or concept of "mental health" was not something I had ever really thought about prior to the accident and I was unprepared for the struggles I went through. When I went to dark places in my mind, I didn't understand. Nor did I know how to control my emotions. I didn't even have access to the language needed to communicate clearly how I was feeling. As a consequence, I became scared of myself and the world around me. All I could do was try to reinforce that protective fortress I'd built as a defense. If I could hide my true feelings or emotions, that made me feel safer.

Statistically, the chance of being injured in a roller coaster accident is only 1 in 24 million, so it's shocking that it happened to me. What is more shocking, however, is how widespread experiences of trauma have become. A recent survey found that a staggering 70 percent of adults in the United States have experienced at least one traumatic event during their lifetimes. That amounts to roughly 223.4 million people—about one in three Americans.

For decades, the term "trauma" has conjured up images of war, violence and terrifying natural disasters, all of which can be incredibly traumatic experiences that impact many people. Consequently, for most of my adolescence to young adulthood, I never considered that what I had experienced was traumatic. I hadn't been to war, I hadn't experienced violence and I hadn't

CONTENTS   xiii

been through a natural disaster—to me, a roller coaster accident didn't "qualify." It wasn't until I was in my early twenties that I was exposed to an expanded idea of trauma and identified that, yes, I had experienced it.

More than ten years after my accident, I gradually began to feel as though I made sense in the world—my feelings of disconnect; the dark, persistent thought patterns; the suffocating long nights of insomnia; and the fragmentation of who I thought I was and who I showed up as all finally began to make sense. I became ravenous for knowledge and information, which led me to my bachelor degree in Applied Science (Psychology). A spring-board that I used to leap into a Graduate Diploma of Counseling. But it wasn't enough—I felt as though I was only touching one side of a multidimensional problem. I went on to become a certi-fied clinical anxiety treatment professional, health and nutrition coach, breathwork teacher and integrative somatic trauma thera-pist (the term "somatic" originates from the Greek word *soma*, meaning "body," and essentially refers to anything relating to—or affecting—the body).

Bringing together all of these science-based modalities, practices, theories and resources that I immersed myself in was an organic process out of which I created a truly integrative and holistic new therapeutic approach for anxiety, stress and trauma. I used this new-found knowledge to gradually understand myself and, over time, bring myself back into my body and reclaim my mental health. Along the way, I insatiably built up my knowledge base, which is now my passion to share.

INTRODUCTION

Welcome to *The Vagus Nerve Reset*. Whatever has brought you here, I hope that the information held within these pages will help you reclaim your sense of self, happiness and vitality. I know how difficult it can be to feel like your past experiences, anxiety and stress are getting the better of you—that hollow feeling that sits within you making everything a question mark in your mind; the exhausting inability to relax, the constant buzz of thoughts and worries; the fatigue that follows you like a dark cloud after almost any social interaction; the feeling of intense overwhelm from certain noises, smells, tastes and sensations; the confusion that comes from being unable to connect your feelings to words; the distance you feel from other people and the world around you, like something has been lost inside of you—I know because I've been there too. But the honest truth is, you have the innate capacity and power to heal and overcome.

By picking up this book, you have taken the first step on your healing journey, embracing the path to somatic (of or relating to the body) therapies, committing to understanding your nervous system and learning how your vagus nerve influences your energy, mood and physical and emotional health every day.

HEALING AND RECOVERY ARE POSSIBLE

Your past experiences are held within your body, physiology and nervous system (which we will build our understanding of in Chapter 1), and your past continues to influence your present *and future* experiences. But you have the power to find the keys to true healing and self-reclamation. In doing so, you will release anxiety, brain fog and imposter syndrome as well as physical issues such as inflammation and gut issues—all of which can be signs of a nervous system out of balance.

Your body has the innate capacity to process, release and return to a state of safety and connection. We have traditionally focused on mind first—the mind being our innate human-ness. Humans are unique because of our ability to be cognitive, right? But what if I told you that we have this "intelligence" the wrong way around? That in order to truly process the ills that arise when we are stuck in our heads, we need to turn inwards and listen to our bodies, and learn to connect to the innate wisdom we hold there. We have to process fully the experiences that have crystallized in our behaviors and caused us so much pain and anguish through trying to "understand" them. What if we could tune into our greatest self-healing power by learning to harness the immense potential of the vagus nerve? To help us consciously and deliberately process, release and heal the stresses and traumas that we have been through? This book will show you how.

As a somatic therapist, I have worked with thousands of people from all over the world who have suffered from chronic anxiety, depression and trauma. Through my journey of self-discovery, I've come to realize that wellness can be achieved in various ways. However, it is through my own painful and traumatic experiences that I have been motivated to seek out a new way of being in the world, a way that is unapologetically vulnerable, yet also authentic and resilient. It became my mission to share, support and guide others to also discover their own truths and sense of self. I have witnessed first-hand how tools and techniques, like the ones I'll teach you in this book, can help you to heal, grow and even flourish. I have had the honor of holding space and watching so many people unfurl and free themselves from their past painful experiences and seemingly never-ending daily symptoms.

So, how did I acquire the skills and knowledge to be able to help so many people? It started with my own experiences.

ABOUT ME

I was in an accident when I was ten years old which changed my life—and altered my nervous system. I shifted from being an outgoing, adventurous and energetic child, to feeling disconnected and constantly at war with my body and mind.

Without having proper understanding, guidance and tools, this led to a chaotic period in young adulthood, leaving me exhausted and frustrated with myself and the mental health system. After an undulating healing journey where, over time, I pieced together my own somatic healing toolkit, I began to use my body as a way of healing what I thought were the problems of my mind. I qualified as a Somatic Healing Practitioner and in this book, you now have access to the incredible healing program I use with my clients.

The moment that changed the course of my life was the moment I learned to consciously bring attention and self-awareness to my physiological experience. Once I began to see my body as a resource and vehicle for processing my emotions— identifying them and giving myself the time and space needed in order for them to emerge naturally rather than trying to suppress or escape whatever those feelings were—I was then able to acknowledge and honor my pain and start my healing journey. Now you can too.

HOW TO USE THIS BOOK

In this book we will explore how our nervous system works and how we can nurture it to positively influence our health, mood and behavior. We will uncover how the nervous system's responses impact our perceptions and learn strategies to redefine these in order to balance those responses and create a new harmonious reality.

In Part 1, we look at the nervous system as a whole, to begin to understand how significantly it influences every bodily system and dictates our mind's landscape, without us even being aware! You will learn about polyvagal theory, the underlying principle of how our nervous system regulates our feelings of safety and consequently how we respond to our experiences in the world. We'll of course meet the star of the show, the vagus nerve, and delve into the detail of exactly what this awe-inspiring nerve network does for our body and mind and how incredible it is that we can consciously choose to soothe our nervous system, as long as we know how. You will begin to learn about the power of somatic healing tools (and what "somatic therapy" is), and the myriad challenges that the modern world presents for our health and well-being. This will give you the foundation of understanding to then be able to confidently move through the healing Vagus Nerve Reset Program (see page 91).

The Reset Program in Part 2 will teach you exactly *how* to access and nurture the systems within you. Learn about the power of breath, touch, movement and intention and how to build these key pillars into your life. The Reset Program shows you how to use these tools on a daily basis, to bring more balance to your every day.

THE INVITATION

What is offered to you in this book is an opportunity to reclaim your space in this world. To reclaim your voice, reclaim ownership over your body, your thoughts, your decisions and the way in which you live.

Living with trauma, stress and/or anxiety can feel as though it robs you of the above. You might have the sensation that you are simply a passenger in your own body. Choices don't feel like real choices, and instead become ultimatums that fill your mind with worry and fear.

Often when we experience big life events, traumatic experiences or chronic and ongoing stress or anxiety, the desire is to return to life "before." To once again be the person you remember yourself to be.

Unfortunately, returning to who you once were is not an option. You are different; you have lived through experiences that have changed you. Perhaps you may be thinking that these experiences have changed you for the worse, but I want you to invite in the idea that, regardless of why or how change has occurred, it is an inevitable part of life.

Every single cell in your body is vibrating and changing as you read this. Tiny cells in your blood live for between 3 and 120 days, while the cells lining your gut live for only about a week. Every single day 330 billion cells in your body are replaced, which is approximately 1 percent of all of the cells that you're made of.

You cannot see this constant renewal, nor can you feel it, but without the ever-present turnover of cells in your body you would no longer be alive.

The "you" that you yearn to return to is no longer physiologically available. So how can you ever reclaim yourself?

The process of reclamation is also a journey of rediscovery. It's the action of releasing and letting go of the idea of who you think you are or used to be, in order to continue to meet yourself again and again.

It's the process of grieving who you once were in order to welcome in who you truly are.

It's the process of reconnecting with parts of yourself that you had written off or kept hidden in order to step into a space of acceptance and compassion.

KNOWLEDGE IS POWER

There is a lot of information in these pages and some of the nervous system detail may feel complex at first. Reread these sections and familiarize yourself with the language and soon it will become something that you instinctively understand as second nature.

While you don't have to be able to remember all of the details, in order for this knowledge to be powerful it needs to be acted on. Yes, knowledge is power—it empowers you to make informed decisions; it enhances your understanding of yourself, others and situations; and ultimately, it increases your chance of being successful in pursuing many of your goals. But that knowledge—and this applies to anything that you learn—can only truly become powerful when there is an action that follows from this expansion.

It is through wholeheartedly immersing yourself in the Reset Program and incorporating these practical exercises regularly that you will grow your connection with your body and explore new ways to heal from trauma, anxiety and stress. This will rekindle your innate capacity to feel safe, secure and at peace with yourself.

The Vagus Nerve Reset is intended to be your resource kit to help you navigate the many challenges of daily life. I'd love you to use it as your companion on your journey, scribble in the margins, highlight what resonates with you, carry it with you as a daily prompt to put yourself first. Consider this book your gateway to a new understanding and appreciation of your body and its incredible ability to heal.

These insights into the inner workings of your nervous system are vital in your progress to healing and overcoming stress, anxiety and trauma. But more importantly, it's going to be the actions that you take in light of this knowledge that will ultimately create powerful shifts in your life.

Although this is a reset program, there is no set time frame; view it as the beginning of a long-term, lifelong commitment to listening to and understanding your body, and forging communication links where they may not currently exist. Remember, there's no need to rush. Take your time as you read, to digest and process all the new ideas and resources.

Make a pact with yourself to return to the book regularly, tracking as the Reset Program outlines, so that you can begin to notice shifts in awareness and experience, and take conscious action on what you are learning. This will ensure that you get the most out of this book and will help you integrate its wisdom into your daily life.

It is my hope that you will find the same freedom and healing that I have experienced on my own journey of discovery. I am here to guide you on this path and hold space for you as we explore what it means to be human, and how we can collectively heal ourselves from trauma, anxiety and stress.

PART 1

YOUR NERVOUS SYSTEM

1.
POLYVAGAL THEORY: THE NEW NERVOUS SYSTEM

Knowing what I know now about my nervous system, if I could go back in time and speak to myself as a ten-year-old in a professional capacity, I would explain that my nervous system was in acute distress. I would tell myself that the nervous system is designed to adapt to our environment and, when it cannot adapt, it goes into survival mode and shuts down. I would explain to myself that this was happening for me in a very real sense every day as my body tried to cope with the pain and shock of the experience and damage I had sustained.

Out of all my injuries and diagnoses, the trauma that had impacted my nervous system was the part of me that went unnoticed, despite the best of intentions. As a result, my physical injuries healed, but the trauma I had experienced remained—leaving me feeling like a stranger in my own body and mind for many years.

Luckily today, we now understand and know how important the nervous system is in healing, regulating and maintaining our health and well-being, and have developed tools and techniques to work with it.

So, let's start to explore our nervous system.

WHAT IS THE NERVOUS SYSTEM?

The nervous system is a web of nerves and specialized cells called neurons that transmit signals throughout the body—it is essentially the body's electrical wiring.

This system carries messages to and from your brain and spinal cord to various parts of your body. You can think of your nervous system like a Wi-Fi network—you can't see it, but it's always there working behind the scenes to make sure that you're able to send and receive messages.

When the network is functioning optimally, the messages being sent are crisp and clear, allowing your heart to beat, your bowel movements to take place regularly and your immune system to fight off infection. You need a solid connection in order for these messages to be sent and received accurately, then necessary change or action is taken by the receiving organ or body part. Every single vital function of the human body is regulated by your nervous system, from your breathing to your heart rate. Without your nervous system, you would simply cease to exist!

Let's geek out a little bit more on the nervous system so we can truly understand what's going on beneath the surface. The nervous system is made up of two structures:

1. **The central nervous system:** this is your brain, spinal cord and nerves.

2. **The peripheral nervous system:** made up of everything outside of your brain and spinal cord.

If we peel the onion another layer further, you can split the peripheral nervous system into two divisions:

2a. **The somatic nervous system:** your *voluntary* division. This is all the nerves that connect the brain and spinal cord to the muscles and sensory receptors in your skin. The somatic nervous system controls all the processes that are managed by you thinking about them, such as walking.

2b. **The autonomic nervous system:** your *involuntary* division. This is where all of the baseline and vital processes of the human body take place; think heartbeat, blood pressure and breathing. All of these processes happen without you having to think about them. They are automatic processes that are regulated—i.e. managed—by the autonomic nervous system.

When we talk about your nervous system in this book, we are talking about the autonomic nervous system (ANS).

The autonomic nervous system: the backbone of life

The ANS is responsible for a large portion of what you feel, express and think and even your behaviors. All of these processes are driven by unconscious patterns: these lie within the ANS and are then expressed externally through automatic responses that you are familiar with in your day-to-day life. Most of the functions of the ANS, such as maintaining and regulating your heart rate, digestion, respiratory rate, sexual arousal, urination and the dilation and contraction of your pupils in your eyes, happen unconsciously. These functions are vital in maintaining your survival and health, and they take place all without you having to think about them (too much).

The ANS is regulated via integrated reflexes through the brain stem, spinal cord and organs. It's also responsible for reflex actions like coughing, swallowing, vomiting and sneezing—all crucial functions of the human body!

Your ANS is tasked with the not-so-basic responsibility of maintaining the state of "homeostasis," which is a fancy word for how our bodies and brains balance all of the different systems within us in order for us to survive and function correctly. The ANS does this by shifting our physiology to adapt to different environments and situations by regulating our internal state, behavior and body movement. For example, if your ANS recognizes that you are too hot, then a number of physiological changes occur (opening up of blood vessels, increased breathing rate—usually through an open mouth—and sweating), which are often coupled with a number of behavioral changes (moving out of the sunshine, splashing cold water on the face, drinking water, and so on). Pretty big job, right?

Like many things in life, it's easy to take our ANS for granted. It's something that we don't have to think about; it ticks along in the background of our lives. And simply because we don't have to pay attention to it in order to breathe and maintain our heartbeat, many of us continue to ignore this complex internal hum.

However, given the widespread effects of this system, it is important to understand what the ANS does and how it influences other aspects of our health, including our cognitive and emotional experience of ourselves and the world around us. Before we dive into that in more detail, let's meet the body's superhighway and the focus of this book—the vagus nerve.

THE VAGUS NERVE

Picture your vagus nerve as a superhighway, carrying information between the brain and internal organs and vice versa to control bodily functions during states of rest and digestion. Made up of thousands of tiny fibers that operate way outside of our consciousness, the vagus nerve is the tenth cranial nerve and is vital in your ability to experience optimal wellness.

The word "vagus" comes from a Latin word meaning "to wander," which is the perfect way to describe it. Your vagus nerve starts in your brain and branches out in multiple directions from the neck to your abdomen. While we commonly refer to the vagus nerve in a singular way, you actually have two vagus nerves—they split from the brain stem and run down the left and right sides of the body respectively. It also has a front (ventral part) and a back (dorsal part):

1. **The ventral (front) vagal pathway** is associated with social engagement, connection and safety. For example, when

you're spending time with people you enjoy and you feel relaxed and comfortable.

2. **The dorsal (back) vagal pathway** is associated with states of shutdown and immobilization, withdrawal, disassociation and disconnection. For example, this can manifest as a feeling of being emotionally detached or disconnected from yourself or your surroundings, similar to a turtle retracting into its shell for protection.

The ventral and dorsal parts form a really important function of the vagus nerve that is vital for our survival—a process called "neuroception."

Neuroception is a neural process in which we subconsciously read cues of danger or safety from our environment. Our brains scan situations and people, making decisions about whether they are safe or dangerous before we even become aware of the judgments made.

This process of neuroception may activate the ventral and/or dorsal parts of the vagus nerve. If your environment and the things within it are sending cues that you are safe, this activates the ventral vagus nerve (front), but if you're receiving cues of potential danger or threat, this will activate the dorsal vagus nerve (back). During neuroception, both may be activated simultaneously as you analyze environmental cues of safety or danger.

Your vagus nerve is like a two-way walkie-talkie—sharing information between your brain (cortex, brain stem and hypothalamus) and your body. But it's not your brain doing most of the talking, it's your body. This is worth thinking about—our body's ability to sense and process information is extraordinary, and most of us are unaware of it. The statistics are striking: your body is sending four times as much information to your brain as your brain is sending to your body. To put that another way, of all the traffic on that superhighway, 80 percent of it—the information coming from your body to your brain—is heading one way, and only 20 percent of the information is coming from your brain to your body!

What's happening in the constant communication between your vagus nerve and your brain? It's a speeded-up version of delivering to the brain what the US military calls a "situation report"—keeping the command center informed about what's happening in the field. Your vagus nerve is busy 24/7 sending messages to let the brain know what's going on throughout the body and in your organs. Think of the phone alert that goes off when you receive a text message. If you could hear the number of messages that your vagus nerve is pinging through to your brain constantly, it would be like white noise—truly gobsmacking.

Now that you understand the powerhouse that is your dedicated vagus nerve, together we're going to get into the nitty-gritty of a new understanding of the ANS, which may get a little "science-y," but just remember, you're innately capable of understanding your brain and body. Let's learn together.

POLYVAGAL THEORY

Traditionally, the nervous system was believed to have two states—one that can either quiet and calm us down (the parasympathetic system), and the other excite or activate us (the sympathetic system)—with heightened activation leading to decreased calm and increased calm leading to decreased activation.

However, polyvagal theory, developed by Dr. Stephen Porges, Professor of Psychiatry and Bioengineering at the University of North Carolina Hospitals in Chapel Hill, puts forward that we are also hardwired with a third type of response: the social engagement system. Polyvagal theory is a groundbreaking theory that explains the role of the nervous system in our behavior, emotions and overall mental health. It explains how our ANS is related to our ability to feel safe and connected in our environment.

Polyvagal theory posits that these three adaptive, innate responses enable our survival: one for safety, one for danger and one for extreme threats. The three adaptive states—and the specific bodily responses they elicit—are expressions of how your ANS interprets safety or danger:

1. **Mobilization**—this is the activation of the sympathetic, fight-or-flight response.

2. **Immobilization**—this is the activation of the dorsal vagal system where you find the freeze, collapse or shutdown response.

3. **Social engagement**—this is your ventral vagal system or parasympathetic nervous system that is activated when you feel relaxed and safe.

In Part 2 we'll explore how you can deepen your awareness of how you move in and out of these different states by mapping your nervous system (see page 138).

But, for now, let's further explore these responses:

Mobilization (fight-or-flight, hyperarousal)

Mobilization is a sympathetic nervous system response that prepares the body for action. It's a whole-body reaction that recruits many organ systems in order to redirect blood so that more oxygen is reaching the areas that need it most during physically demanding moments. It is most commonly known as the "fight-or-flight" response because, in moments of need, it prepares the body to either fight off a threat or run away from it. The mobilization response is not a bad thing: we use it when we need to exert physical energy; for example, when we play sports, laugh and play. It becomes unhelpful when the mobilization system is activated in the absence of real threat, like when we are stuck in traffic or our email inboxes are overflowing with messages.

Long-term activation of the mobilization response is called hyperarousal and may cause symptoms such as:

- agitation, irritability or frustration
- feeling restless and/or fidgeting, unable to sit still
- feeling like you need to escape
- physical aggression or feelings of anger
- hypervigilance, looking for risks or possible danger
- inability to focus or concentrate
- unwanted and intrusive thoughts
- feelings of fear, anxiety or stress

Immobilization (shutdown, dorsal vagal, hypoarousal)

In evolutionary terms, the immobilization response is our oldest and most primitive survival response. However, in modern life we can also go into shutdown mode when faced with extreme stress or trauma, burnout or overwhelming tasks such as a big work presentation. When the body and mind become overloaded and overwhelmed they can enter this state of immobilization, also referred to as hypoarousal.

Dorsal vagal, or hypoarousal can make us feel like our world has shrunk, that nothing is interesting or engaging anymore. Furthermore, we may not even be able to summon the energy needed for basic daily tasks such as getting up in the morning.

It may look like:

- a "freeze" response
- feeling numb, dissociated or disconnected
- daydreaming or "zoning out"
- brain fog and/or exhaustion
- dulled senses
- being very quiet or withdrawn
- socially isolating yourself
- finding it difficult to make decisions
- difficulty remembering events or things

If we take a look at how animals react to danger, we can see that they tend to "shake off" the "freeze" response caused by an external threat. This shaking is the animal's means of releasing any pent-up energy brought on by danger. If in any way or form the animal is not allowed to release this stored energy, they are at risk of dying.

We humans are slightly different from animals in the wild in that we have many different physiological response systems that can be deployed when we feel under threat. If a traumatic event poses a threat to a person's safety, for example, this creates a physical and emotional reaction within the individual that activates either the sympathetic nervous system—"mobilization"— or the dorsal vagal—"immobilization"—response, both of which are necessary for survival.

However, when the nervous system becomes unable to complete its natural, survival-based response—for example, if someone is held against their will, an individual is physically immobilized or even if we are in a social situation that does not allow for the natural expression of these responses—the negative experience can become stored in the body, resulting in several emotional and physiological problems.

Ventral vagal (parasympathetic)

When the ventral vagus response is activated, you will feel relaxed and at ease. This can manifest itself in many ways—a smile that comes naturally to your face when meeting new people or feeling more connected with loved ones, for example. This might also look like mindfulness, compassion, curiosity and calm. The activation of this part of our nervous system allows us a break from the tension associated with the fight-or-flight responses (like anxiety).

Each of the above systems can be triggered by changes in what we see in our environment as well as inner shifts at any given moment (which we'll explore in the next chapter)—and are regulated by the vagus nerve. A healthy vagus nerve keeps you calm in stressful situations and lets you know when danger is gone. This allows your body to rest and repair itself.

The vagus nerve also plays several other crucial roles:

- It regulates a stable heart rate and prevents unhealthily irregular heart rhythms. It accomplishes this by secreting acetylcholine, a substance that slows down electrical impulses in the heart and in turn decreases its beating rate. This reduces your energy expenditure and also helps you feel calm and relaxed.

- It oversees digestion. Your vagus nerve regulates the release of digestive enzymes as well as the movement of food through your digestive tract. It also acts as the communication link between your gut and your brain, and it signals when you're feeling full after eating a meal. The health of your gut and digestive system can have a significant impact on your emotional and mental health. When your gut is content and healthy, this keeps your vagus nerve happy, as well as your brain.

- It assists with the release of insulin from the pancreas and the production of bile from the liver. All of this allows you to gain important nutrients from your food, which gives you energy, strength and vitality, as well as expelling waste and any unwanted nasties from your body.

- It regulates the muscles in your neck and throat to allow you to swallow and talk, which enables you to communicate effectively with others.

- It controls inflammation so that you are able to maintain a healthy immune system.
- It carries sensory information from the skin of the ear to the brain, allowing you to hear and process sounds.
- It plays a major role in keeping your immune system in good order by regulating the production of antibodies.
- It controls the muscles in your eyes and face to allow you to blink, smile or frown, enabling you to connect with others, make eye contact and change your facial expression.
- It allows you to tune into other people's voices and notice any alterations in their tones, too.

The vagus nerve is also the body's main channel for relaying information about lung and airway conditions to the brain. It controls breathing and other respiratory functions, and provides information from the lungs to your brain about how well you are breathing—so that signals can be sent back to control the rate of respiration accordingly. As you'll come to see in the Reset Program, your breath is one of the only automatic functions you have access to that can massively influence and shift your ANS, and is the most effective and immediate way of connecting to your vagus nerve—and you do it every minute of every day!

Your vagus nerve is incredibly important when it comes to your day-to-day life. Without it, you wouldn't be able to swallow that delicious cup of coffee in the morning or connect with your loved ones through eye contact. In order to carry out these many duties, the vagus nerve needs to be healthy (I am going to share plenty of ways to achieve this in the Reset Program in Part

2). You can assess the health of your vagus nerve by measuring how well your vagus nerve handles all the activity it's responsible for. It's time to talk about vagal tone.

VAGAL TONE

Vagal tone is a fancy way of measuring how well your vagus nerve is functioning, and it's an indication of whether you are able to bounce back from stress. It also helps you understand your capacity for self-regulation and how you respond to the world around you. Your vagal tone is a reflection of the state of your nervous system, which includes everything from how well your heart rate and breathing are regulated to how much you feel calm or stressed out in any given moment.

Your vagal tone is influenced by many factors, including genetics, lifestyle choices, diet and environment. It's important to note that your vagal tone is not a permanent state and you can learn how to improve your vagal tone naturally—which we'll come to explore in Part 2.

Perhaps surprisingly, vagal tone can be assessed indirectly through something called heart rate variability (HRV), which is the measure of how much time elapses between individual heartbeats. These fluctuations are very small—typically a fraction of a second. The time between one heartbeat and the next changes a lot from beat to beat and moment to moment. We actually want a lot of variation in the timing of our heartbeats, because that's what gives us our ability to respond flexibly to the ever-changing circumstances of life.

Your heart beats at a certain rate, and it adapts depending on what you're doing at each moment of the day. Your heart will beat more slowly when you're in a calm, relaxed state. On the flip side, your heart rate increases when you're exercising or experiencing stress. It's important to note here that if you have any concerns about your heart rate, please see a doctor.

Your heart rate also varies depending on the demands of your body and other factors like your breathing patterns. Your HRV can also be impacted by things like medications or medical devices, such as pacemakers (devices that are placed in the chest to correct heart problems). As you age, your overall HRV will naturally decrease over time.

Your remarkable body has evolved over time with incredible adaptations to ensure your survival through diverse situations and challenges. Your HRV is a reflection of how well and how quickly your body can adjust to changing circumstances and stressors. High HRV generally means that your body is highly adaptive to many different changes and experiences. Usually individuals with high HRV are more resilient to stressful experiences and also report a greater sense of well-being.

In general, lower HRV can be a sign of a less resilient nervous system, with a lower capacity to handle changing situations and can be an indicator of future health issues. Less variability between heartbeats actually signals that there is an imbalance in your ANS, or sympathetic dominance.

Individuals who have higher resting heart rates tend to have lower HRV, due to their heart beating faster, meaning there is less time in between each beat of the heart and therefore less of an opportunity for variability.

When your vagus nerve and ventral vagal system are functioning optimally and your system is in a relaxed state, the variation between your heartbeats is greater.

Essentially, your HRV is a marker of how well you cope with stress and change, and how accessible and easy it is for you to return to your ventral vagal system after facing challenges.

MEASURING HEART RATE VARIABILITY

Measuring HRV at home can be tricky because the variations in timing of your heartbeats are microseconds. The most accurate way to measure HRV is through specialized medical machines like electrocardiograms (ECG), which have the power to measure the electrical activity of your heart through sensors attached to your chest. Other medical devices—like heart monitors that track HRV over longer periods of time—also give extremely accurate readings.

However, access to these medical technologies can be expensive or may not be available for the purpose of gathering information on your physiological functioning. Thanks to advances in modern technology, there are now a number of at-home devices that do have the capacity to track HRV. For example, heart rate monitors that are strapped around the chest are often used by athletes to measure HRV. These devices are relatively new, and are becoming a more affordable and accessible option.

Additionally, some smart devices, like smart watches, also have the capacity to calculate HRV, although these readings are less accurate than those of medical machines like ECGs.

Vagal tone is a physical and emotional barometer that gives us insight into our physical and emotional health. Low vagal tone is often a sign that your nervous system isn't functioning at its best and can be reflected in many ways such as:

- Crohn's disease
- irritable bowel syndrome/disease
- Parkinson's disease
- epilepsy
- type 2 diabetes
- high blood pressure
- cardiovascular disease
- anxiety
- depression
- post-traumatic stress disorder

On the flipside, high vagal tone (high HRV) is associated with a happy, healthy and optimally functioning vagus nerve. This helps us feel relaxed and calm in the face of stress, lowers our heart rate when we're feeling threatened or nervous, and regulates our breathing so we can think clearly during stressful moments. A healthy vagus nerve also fosters empathy for others, forming a bridge between them and you based on your common humanity. It is commonly called the "love nerve" because, when activated by an empathetic person, you love more easily and unconditionally. If you've ever been in the presence of someone and it literally feels like they just melt away all of your worries and stress, this is the work of your ventral vagus nerve! Increasing your vagal tone activates the ventral vagal response, which means your body can relax more quickly after stressful situations.

We want our vagus nerve to be strong and healthy, so whenever we do have the opportunity to sit in that connected, calm and grounded place, we can access it easily. It's reassuring to know that you can improve your vagal tone. Stimulating the nerve helps people leave "fight-or-flight" and enter into a safer state—like social engagement.

Throughout the Reset Program in Part 2 you're going to be learning how to do exactly that through movement, reconnective practices and gentle lifestyle shifts. These will expand and build natural resilience into your nervous system, widening your tolerance, capacity and control over your life.

Once you understand how to nurture and work with the vagus nerve, your inner healer will be unleashed. But before we dive deeper into that, it's important to set the scene a bit more. In the next chapter, I'll explain how the three systems of your nervous system work together and what happens when we get "stuck" in one state.

2.
HOW THE NERVOUS SYSTEM WORKS

In this chapter we'll further explore the three states your nervous system can be in according to polyvagal theory. With this knowledge, you'll learn how to identify which state you're in and then use the skills and strategies outlined in the Reset Program to take charge of your nervous system and shift it into a state of safety.

VENTRAL VAGAL (PARASYMPATHETIC) ACTIVATION: REST AND DIGEST, FRIEND OR FAWN

When there is a perceived threat or danger present, your nervous system uses the sympathetic (fight-or-flight) or dorsal vagal (freeze or shutdown) responses to keep you safe. The social engagement system operates slightly differently to these survival systems. To access and use the social engagement system, a sense of safety is necessary.

As you learned in the previous chapter, there are two vagus nerves—these branch off on the left and right sides of your body. The dorsal branch of the vagus nerve is responsible for primal survival functions, like shutting down or collapsing. This branch of the vagus nerve affects organs below the diaphragm (a large, dome-shaped muscle that sits below the heart and lungs and is attached to the rib cage and spine), as well as the heart and lungs.

The ventral branch of the vagus nerve—part of a system that regulates social engagement and other bodily functions—affects bodily functions above the diaphragm.

The ventral vagal branch has the capacity to create activation of the body and mind in a far more nuanced way. Unlike sympathetic activation, which is often intense and always coupled with the release of cortisol and adrenaline, the ventral vagal pathway can create subtle activation that is chemical-free, allowing you to adjust your physiological state quickly when engaging with others.

You have experienced this type of ventral vagal activation in your own life, for example when you feel that excited energy just from being around your friends or doing an activity that you love. When we feel safe in our environment, we are able to interact with others appropriately—moving from excitement and energy to empathetic and grounded effortlessly.

Your social engagement system operates via the vagus nerve, which influences and promotes connection and relationships by simultaneously activating and calming us—making it possible to navigate social interactions successfully.

Humans are biologically and evolutionarily hardwired as

social creatures. Our survival as a species has been intricately tied to our ability to work together and build social connections. In fact, the most recent research suggests that human beings have evolved a "social brain" whose primary function is to keep us connected with others (the social engagement system).

Babies use crying to gain attention from caregivers, and this allows them to not only gain nourishment, but also safety in knowing that they are protected.

As infants continue to grow and develop, so too does their attachment. They begin to broaden and expand who they interact with outside of their primary caregivers, often smiling and interacting with strangers.

As children continue to develop, these attachments increase too. They form protective bonds with "safe" individuals to maintain their safety and have their basic needs met.

This resource is similarly expressed in adults. We may reach out to trusted friends, family or others in times of need or crisis to feel secure and supported. For example, if you are driving and get a flat tire, you might phone a family member for help.

As humans, this "friend" response helps ensure our survival. Making friends with others allows us to create a sort of safety net—people around us who have our backs. They also offer fulfillment of our needs—a sense of belonging, love and affection, intimacy and connection. They form our social engagement system. When we are connected with others who make us feel safe, connected and supported, we are operating in our ventral vagal system.

The friend response, sometimes called the "fawn" response, is also used when we feel threatened or in danger. We may use this response to try to befriend, flatter or make ourselves useful to others when we feel tension or pressure. For example, if someone is quick to anger when the house is messy, we may go above and beyond to make sure that everything is in place before they get home. Or we may apologize profusely for something that wasn't necessarily our fault, in order to maintain peace.

The friend response is used both in moments of perceived danger and in times of social connection and engagement.

When I talk about social connection and engagement, I am not talking about how many followers you have on social media or the number of likes and comments you get when you post a photo. What I mean is our ability to have positive interactions with others and the world around us. Yes, this can include the interactions you have online, depending on the relationship that has been cultivated.

Individuals who feel socially connected and have strong, mutual and respectful relationships with trusted others tend to have better mental health outcomes and overall well-being than those who are not socially connected.

While connection can be a powerful experience, it can also be difficult to find or maintain in our busy lives. It's also important to understand that individuals experiencing mental health issues often have a harder time connecting with others, but this can be particularly true for those who have experienced trauma. Research shows that individuals who experience trauma may have difficulty trusting others or feeling safe in close relationships. This can make it difficult to build strong social connections and experience the benefits of social support.

Despite the challenges we may currently feel when it comes

to creating and maintaining strong social connections, it's important to remember that we can all do it.

In fact, as you learned in Chapter 1, you are wired in a way that makes connection inevitable—through your vagus nerve. When the vagus nerve is activated, we begin to operate in a ventral vagal system—the social engagement system.

When the social engagement system is activated, we feel safe and connected with others, making us more likely to produce appropriate facial cues—like smiling—and enhancing our ability to hear and speak fluently.

We can utilize the social engagement system in our own healing journey both as a resource to regulate our nervous system, but also as a tool to maintain positive mental health in the long term. Engaging social systems and creating connections is an important part of the recovery process, particularly when it comes to experiencing a sense of belonging and building out your support networks.

MOBILIZATION (SYMPATHETIC ACTIVATION): FIGHT-OR-FLIGHT

When the sympathetic nervous system is activated, the body enters a state of mobilization, or fight-or-flight.

The *fight response* is a survival response that is often deployed if social engagement has not been effective in reducing or eliminating the threat or danger.

This response system demands high energy expenditure and often manifests as physically making yourself bigger: puffing out your chest and standing up tall to make yourself look more imposing. It can be demonstrated in overt aggression such as yelling or physical altercations, or more subtly through tone of voice, cadence (speed) of speech and language used.

The aim of the *flight response* is to create as much space between the potential threat or danger and you. This could look like actually fleeing or running from one area to another, or moving to a place that you think is suitable to hide in.

Like the fight response, the flight response uses a lot of energy in the body, with glucose stores being freed up so that there's more energy being supplied to muscles and adrenaline circulating the body so that your blood flows to big muscle groups and your lungs have greater capacity.

If you've ever been chased in a game you may have felt that rush of adrenaline that allowed you to run just that extra bit faster than you would normally. This is made possible by these physiological changes that are happening within your body without you even knowing.

IMMOBILIZATION (DORSAL VAGAL ACTIVATION): SHUTDOWN/FREEZE

When your brain and body have realized that befriending, fighting or fleeing from a threat are not working or will not work, it automatically shifts down a gear into a freeze response.

Freeze response can be thought of as an overwhelming of the nervous system, pushing your brain and body to downregulate the nervous system into a depressed "frozen" state. This is where the parasympathetic nervous system spikes and takes over from the sympathetic nervous system, slowing the whole system down.

In response to any number of triggers—including fear, anxiety and panic—we may freeze in our everyday lives. The freeze response can be activated for any number of reasons. For example, while giving an important presentation at work, talking to people we find intimidating (such as bosses), dealing with social and relational conflicts, being in a situation that we find scary (like driving at night) and even being generally overwhelmed by the demands of life.

Any time that your brain and body become overwhelmed and feel as though the only way to protect you is to completely shut down is when the freeze response will be deployed. Everything from accidents, medical incidents and surgeries, receiving painful or difficult news, grief and loss, bad break-ups and being bullied—especially if under prolonged circumstances—can activate the freeze response.

This response system is almost always evident in those who have experienced forms of sexual abuse because this protective state leaves the body and mind "frozen," releasing endogenous opioids into the body that have a numbing effect, reducing pain and subduing the mind.

The freeze response often has shame or guilt attached to it, coupled with feelings of *Why didn't I do something?* But the truth is, as we have seen, these responses are involuntary and automatic.

The freeze response is also an extremely useful response to support you getting through horrific experiences. Its ultimate goal is to protect you and help you survive the ordeal so that you have the best opportunity to recover. This may be experienced as feelings of defeat and hopelessness, shame, numbness, a depressed energy (low), derealization (feeling disconnected from the world), depersonalization (feeling like you're not real) and dissociation (separating the body and mind), as well as altered states of consciousness (drifting off into an imaginary world or reality) or total loss of consciousness (passing out or fainting).

IS ONE RESPONSE "BETTER" THAN THE OTHERS?

If we look at the purpose or function of each of our survival responses, we'll see that they all serve to protect us in some way. For instance, if you're being chased by a lion, it's probably not a good idea to flee—this might make things worse. However, upon hearing an alarm sounding for the first time in many years, I would imagine that most people would have an instant "flight" response triggered without thinking about it.

Like a grandfather clock that has a pendulum swinging back and forth, so too does your nervous system. It's in constant motion, adapting to the current environment, stressor or event that is in front of it. It needs to have the capacity to move quickly in and out of nervous system states like fight-or-flight, freeze or into ventral vagal. This is your nervous system being extremely good at surviving.

Ideally, the three states of your nervous system work together in this way—allowing you to masterfully navigate life and the potential challenges that come up day to day. The ANS is similar to a scale—like Bonnie and Clyde or yin and yang, the branches of your ANS work together to create this balance.

The hypothalamus is a region of your brain that processes information and sends signals to other parts of the body. The ANS provides those instructions—either prompting activation or relaxation, depending on whether it detects danger or safety. It responds not only to what you ate for lunch or that difference of opinion with a co-worker, but also to the exciting news that you just got a promotion or arriving home to a welcome surprise, like your house has been cleaned for you.

If you think back to the last time that you heard a loud noise at night, you may have noticed that your heart rate kicked up a notch—this is your fight-or-flight (sympathetic) system coming online, releasing adrenaline and cortisol into the body to increase blood flow to muscles in case they need it. Or maybe when you heard that loud noise you froze and stayed very still in your bed—this is your freeze (dorsal vagal) system coming online, releasing endorphins into the body to increase your tolerance to pain and decrease breathing and heart rate.

Once the fear subsides and you realize that you're safe, the fight-or-flight or freeze system starts to quieten down and your ventral vagal (parasympathetic) system takes the lead in bringing about a return to normal functioning. It tells your heart rate to slow back down and lowers blood pressure. It also signals to various systems of your body to relax or revert back to the state they were in before the loud noise.

Your fight-or-flight system is the accelerator or gas pedal; it takes the wheel when you're faced with stress and challenges.

Your ventral vagal system is your brake, slowing down the onslaught of adrenaline and cortisol.

Your dorsal vagal system is the emergency "off" switch; it slows you down, or even stops you completely, when things get too intense.

When we are emotionally healthy, we are able to move freely between each of these states and not get "stuck" in one. However, chronic stress or trauma can interfere with our body's ability to assess situations and respond appropriately, keeping us from recognizing when a situation is safe. This sets off a vicious cycle—when our nervous systems don't realize it's not an emergency anymore, our bodies stay in fight-or-flight or freeze mode continuously—whether there are real threats around or not. In the absence of safety, our bodies get stuck in a state of defense and, when our self-defense systems are chronically activated, it reduces our ability to connect and communicate with others in effective and restorative ways. Being in one state also prevents you from using the behaviors associated with another. If, for example, you are in a fight-or-flight state (you're afraid), then being in that state will prevent your ability to socially engage.

If there are ongoing, chronic or underlying unprocessed experiences or stressors in your life, it's like having your foot to the floor on the accelerator all of the time.

Over time, your ventral vagal nervous system gets quieter and harder to access, especially in moments when you desperately need to rest. Your ventral vagal system is like a muscle that needs to be trained in order to grow. But if the sympathetic nervous system is always the one in the gym, then it never gets a chance to be worked out and gets smaller and smaller over time.

THE PHYSIOLOGY OF ANXIETY, STRESS AND TRAUMA

We've all felt it—that uncomfortable, pervasive fear that feels like it could swallow us whole.

To experience anxiety is to be human. Every single human on earth will feel a sense of anxiety at some point in their lives because, at its core, anxiety is survival. It's an innate, inbuilt and evolutionary response system that everyone is prewired to have within them in order to survive in this world.

You may have heard anxiety explained as an evolutionary hangover from when our ancestors had to run from lions or saber-toothed tigers. I tend to disagree with this view. I believe humans to be extremely adaptive to their environments and if experiencing anxiety wasn't beneficial to our survival, then this response system would surely have diminished over the thousands of years of evolution.

But still, anxiety remains a strong physiological pathway within each of us, and if you look around twenty-first-century society, it's not difficult to understand why this response system remains necessary to our survival.

If you take a typical day from your own life, there are many activities that might cause anxiety—for example, crossing a busy road, driving a car or interacting with many different people with whom you are unfamiliar. These normal, mundane activities all require—on some level—attention to potential harm or quickly changing situations.

While you may not be exposed to being chased by a saber-toothed tiger, you *are* exposed to traffic, deadlines, financial pressures, environmental toxins, poor sleep, lack of support, a loss of belonging, the continual alerts of social media, news notifications and text messages, as well as chronic stress and traumatic experiences. These all require your body and mind to respond in some way in order to survive.

Anxiety is a physiological survival response. It enacts changes to your body, mind and behaviors. This is experienced both in humans and animals in response to anything that could potentially threaten well-being or survival—whether that's actual, potential or even purely imagined.

Anxiety is often termed as a mental health issue, but in reality, it is our inbuilt alarm system. The experience of fear or worry isn't confined to your thoughts—you literally physically feel it—the trembling in your hands, the intense racing of your heart, headaches that come from nowhere, and that urgent need to go to the bathroom. This is your body responding to feeling threatened. It's an "all systems go" experience.

Your digestive system grinds to a halt because, well, eating is not a very good survival tactic! Maybe you have felt your mouth and throat go so dry that it's almost impossible to talk. Or maybe you've felt a wave of nausea wash over you, like a stone is sitting in your belly. Maybe you've even had that gut-wrenching emergency need to get to the toilet as soon as possible.

Similarly, you've probably experienced that buzzing, amped up energy that courses through your body. Maybe you've noticed yourself bouncing your foot or leg up and down. Adrenaline and cortisol begin to flood through your body to make sure that your muscles are prepared and ready to either fight off attackers or run as fast as you can away from them.

To survive the ever-changing landscape of life, all humans possess inbuilt survival responses that help them navigate it. It is often the case that survival responses are feared or stigmatized, but your experience of being a survivor is valid in every way, and you have done exactly what you had to in every moment to survive. Your brain and body are designed to survive, so by deploying these survival responses, you are actually functioning correctly in that moment of threat or perceived danger, even if those responses turn out not to be required and it was a false alarm.

Whichever response you use at any given moment is the one that is most likely to promote survival. So, in essence, your responses are equally valuable and helpful to you in supporting your ability to deal with life events, trauma or challenges.

More than once I've had clients or individuals remark, "You must be so calm all the time!"—and honestly, this couldn't be further from the truth. Just like you, I go through periods that can be majorly stressful. I get triggered, argue with my husband and, some days, I'm just in a plain filthy mood! I, like you, am a human being, and let's be real—being a human in the twenty-first century can be pretty damn stressful.

It's normal for you and every single other person on this planet to have moments of stress, anxiety, fear and any other emotion besides a tranquil feeling of calm. But if an individual's system is thrown out of balance for any reason—physical, emotional or psychological—those survival responses may start to show up in everyday life situations—like when someone doesn't respond to your text message quickly and your thoughts begin to negatively spiral, or if you get stuck in traffic and you feel a sense of panic rising. Sometimes a survival response can pop up seemingly out of nowhere—where no threat actually exists. In the extreme form of this, it can feel like there is no "off" switch for these survival responses.

What are emotions?

The term "emotion" can be difficult to clarify. In scientific language, emotions are often referred to as "affect," which are the strong feelings that you may have based on your circumstances, moods or relationships with others.

Essentially, emotions are responses that people have to events or situations. What emotion a person feels is determined by the event or situation itself. For example, you may feel excited when you receive a job offer, but you feel fear when something threatens you or your well-being in some way.

There is also a physiological aspect to emotion. Every emotion creates a sensation or feeling within the body—from butterflies in your stomach when you're excited to sweaty palms when you're nervous.

Your emotional experience has a massive influence over how you connect with others, the way in which you solve problems and your ability to focus and be attentive.

"Positive" emotions such as love, joy, hope and confidence engage you with the external, outside world and those within it.

When you are engaged with the outside world, you connect to yourself and those around you in a grounded and mindful way. This broadens your ability to seek even more positive emotions or roll with life's punches when challenges arise.

When you feel afraid, ashamed or despairing, your world shrinks. You become less inclined to open yourself up to connective experiences and people. Your mind becomes preoccupied with reducing risk or exposure so that you are less likely to notice opportunities for connection with other people. In parallel, your ability to connect with yourself shrinks too.

Traumatic events can flood a person's system with negative emotions, like anxiety or rage. These emotions are powerful and can be overwhelming. They can also be very limiting. When these negative emotions get stuck in your system, they have a tendency to distort or even shut down your ability to think clearly about what is happening in the moment—and this can make it difficult to respond effectively.

How the brain processes trauma

A beautiful explanation to help expand your understanding of the experience of trauma is:

TRAUMA IS ANYTHING THAT IS TOO MUCH, TOO FAST, TOO SOON.
Peter Levine

All being well, once the threat or danger has passed, the brain and body should come back to a state of optimal, ventral vagal calm. In this state, you are able to process the world around you with a wide range of sensory information and come up with a variety of solutions that employ creative reasoning and logic.

Unfortunately, when a traumatic event occurs, the natural movement back into the ventral vagal state can be thwarted. You may find yourself stuck in an activated, reactive or depressed (shutdown) state. In my roller coaster accident, I was literally trapped, so my body and nervous system were unable to return to a natural state of balance.

You may have heard of the work of doctors Peter Levine, Bessel van der Kolk and Dan Siegel, among others, who have dedicated their lives to exploring the impact of trauma on our bodies. They have found that trauma impacts our nervous systems at all levels. This can be as little as a minor bump in your day that triggers negative thoughts and emotions, but then leads you down a path of internal chaos until you've calmed yourself down again—which can take days or even months.

When a person experiences trauma in any form, the nervous system gets stretched beyond its capacity to regulate itself. For some individuals, the nervous system becomes stuck in the "on" position, and they become overstimulated and unable to relax. This state—the hyperarousal that we explored on page 19—is physiologically stressful and taxing for every system of the body. As we've seen, short-term activation of the fight-or-flight system is necessary and life-saving, but it's not designed to continue over long periods of time. This is because it uses a lot of energy to remain in this state. It also impacts other functions like sleep, focus and the ability to assess risks and make healthy decisions.

The experience of trauma does not always cause a state of

hyperarousal however. It can also cause the nervous system to tip into the freeze state (dorsal vagal—see page 20), which can lead to depression, dissociation, disconnection and fatigue.

Some individuals can alternate between these nervous system states of high arousal and low shutdown responses.

Research has also found that specific areas in the brain can be impacted by traumatic stress:

- **The amygdala** is a brain region that plays a critical role in the formation of memories—traumatic stress may lead to increased and overactive amygdala function.
- **The hippocampus** is a brain region that plays a major role in learning and memory—traumatic stress may lead to decreased hippocampal function.
- **The prefrontal cortex** is a brain region that plays an important role in complex cognitive processes such as decision-making, planning, problem-solving, creativity and impulse control—traumatic stress may lead to decreased function in the prefrontal cortex.

The amygdala, which plays a role in the emotional response to stimuli, and the hippocampus, which is responsible for forming memories, are thought to be particularly susceptible to the adverse effects of traumatic stress. The outcome can be changes in behavior, mood and physical health.

The physical effects of stress and trauma

A network of structures in the brain known as the "default mode network" (DMN) or "default state network"' plays a critical role in human thought, perception and behavior. The DMN is involved in awareness of your own internal sensations, coordinating emotions and thoughts, and reflecting on yourself—your emotional state and physical condition.

Brain scans of post-traumatic stress disorder (PTSD) patients show that those areas of their brain involved in sensing internal state and emotions under-activate—shifting into low gear to help them avoid feeling trauma's uncomfortable, painful effects.

One of the effects of shutting down the DMN is diminished awareness and sensation in your body.

For some individuals who experience trauma, their DMN may overreact to certain internal physical sensations. For example, a survivor who experiences shallow breathing as a mild stressor could find themselves going rapidly from shallow breathing to having a panic attack.

The physical effects of stress, trauma and emotions are not confined to the mind; they involve changes in hormones, muscular contractions throughout the body, heart rate and breathing—all of which influence how we sense ourselves.

As a result of trauma or traumatic life events (remember, trauma is anything that occurs too much, too fast or too soon) the negative emotions that accompany such events can become trapped in the body, resulting in the nervous system becoming stuck in survival mode.

Learning how to sense and interpret internal body sensations correctly is a critical part of the healing process. To get back into your body and be able to move again, the first step you must take is to gently guide yourself back to safety. A lot of the work we'll do in this book will help you to find the control panel for your own internal guidance system and rebuild a foundation of safety within. Only then can you recognize and regain control over your survival responses—known as "regulation," which we'll explore in the next chapter.

3.
REGULATING THE NERVOUS SYSTEM

You wake up feeling rested ... Like a warm hug, waves of connection and safety are felt throughout your whole body. A sense of calmness washes through you, your mind is present, noticing shifts, changes and sensations, but you're not distracted. You stay even-tempered, you can handle constructive criticism and remain calm in the face of any challenges.

In this beautifully regulated state, you handle the stresses of your commute and daily responsibilities with ease. Stuck in traffic? *No problem—I'll just make a phone call to let work know I'll be late.* Spill coffee all over yourself? *Well, that happens sometimes!*

You feel confident and satisfied after dealing with the challenges of a tough day, so you relax and prepare to deal with whatever comes your way tomorrow.

Let's flip that for a moment.

Imagine you have the worst night's sleep ... Every hour you check your phone in the dark, getting more and more frustrated with your lack of sleep. When you eventually get out of bed, it feels as though your eyes are hanging out of your head. You seem to be moving at a snail's pace.

You get into your car and, as you're closing the door, it bumps your elbow, so then you spill some of your coffee on the sleeve of your top. You grit your teeth and take a deep breath.

You sit in the morning commute of bumper-to-bumper traffic, the whites of your knuckles showing as you grip the steering wheel tightly. *It could be worse,* you tell yourself.

Tense after your commute, you arrive at work and someone makes a joke remark. *They're having a dig at me!* That's it! You can't handle any more—you feel your blood begin to boil and redness creeps up your neck. You snap back at them sharply, making that person shrink away.

The rest of your day seems to follow suit—you go from one issue to the next. When you get in your car to head home, you feel overwhelmed and stressed thinking about all the things you didn't get done.

The twang of guilt for how you treated people and handled situations plays on repeat in your mind as you switch on the TV to relax. But you can't wind down; your mind feels like a radio station switching from one channel to the next.

You just need to sleep, so you jump into bed, only to find yourself lying there wide awake.

Not such a great day, right?

Do you recognize yourself in either of the above scenarios? We've all been there, whether we've been on top of the world or walking around with a short fuse, and both are great examples of the different states of your nervous system in action in everyday life.

What polyvagal theory puts forward is that biological shifts, reactions and assessments of the safety of the environment come first—this essentially means that changes occur first within the body and the nervous system. For example, when you get startled by a loud noise, your sympathetic nervous system jumps into action and cortisol floods the body making your heart beat faster. These body-level changes then influence things like our emotions (fear), thoughts (*What if something bad is about to happen?*), feelings (nervousness, dread), behaviors (jumping up and moving to a different area) and sensations (tingling, buzzing, dizziness).

We can use this knowledge that the body comes first to begin to rewire the nervous system so that it changes the way we experience and respond to stress and achieve greater connection, safety and resilience. When we learn to work with our bodies, we begin to also change the way that we think, feel and behave.

In a therapeutic setting, polyvagal theory focuses on the body's nervous system, its states and how it responds to stress. It emphasizes the importance of physiological safety in order to create an emotional sense of safety and aims to teach individuals to regulate their nervous system function in order to create balance between the three adaptive systems.

A regulated nervous system is not a nervous system that is always calm or one that never ever gets activated or dips into a freeze state. Quite often, there is a misconception that, once you have regulated your nervous system—*dusts hands off*—you're done, you are now magically calm, even when there is a hell-storm going on around you.

Unfortunately, this is not the case, and I want to reframe the term "nervous system regulation" for you in a way that can help you understand why you wouldn't even want to be calm all the time!

WHAT IS NERVOUS SYSTEM REGULATION?

At its core, a regulated nervous system is a resilient nervous system. The definition of resilience is the ability to bounce back, even flourish, after challenges or difficult experiences. A well regulated nervous system has a large capacity for interpersonal relationships. You can deal with small mistakes or challenges without getting overwhelmed by them and stay grounded in the present moment. It facilitates connection, problem-solving coupled with realistic action and a certain amount of letting go of what is outside of your control.

Regulation isn't in fact being in a calm ventral vagal state all of the time. It's the ability to shift between different levels of arousal as necessary in response to stressors.

Our ability to cope with change means that, when we encounter a stressful situation, we can adjust and adapt so that we are not overwhelmed. It also means that, after the stressor has passed, our bodies return to normal function.

This ability to be flexible and adapt to circumstances gives us a sense of agency; it makes us feel confident because we can navigate the world in ways that make sense.

When our nervous system is resilient, being in our bodies fosters a feeling of safety. We are able to notice when we are in a state of activation or depression and use our resources to support our nervous systems to gently come back to a calm and grounded state.

On the flip side, you could say that nervous system dysregulation is an overwhelmed nervous system. It translates to a feeling of helplessness or powerlessness. You might feel as though you have zero control over how you respond to triggers and that you often feel "stuck" either in an activated or deactivated state even long after the trigger has been removed.

Going through life with a nervous system that is dysregulated is like walking on a tightrope that has a frayed line. With each step, "ping," another piece of the rope is severed, making the journey frightening and dangerous. Everything that comes remotely close to you has the potential to make you fall off that rope, so you close off to connection, you feel irritated and exhausted; all of your energy is focused on staying "safe."

If our nervous system is chronically dysregulated, we may feel pain or discomfort in our bodies. Our entire experience of being alive can become frightening. Trauma, burnout, illness and chronic pain are all manifestations of a stressed nervous system.

WHAT DOES A DYSREGULATED NERVOUS SYSTEM LOOK LIKE?

Your body handles all sorts of challenges, changes, risks and stressors on a daily basis. But when things in life get chaotic—you're under a tremendous amount of stress, you barely get any sleep, the food you eat isn't giving you the nutrients you need, a relationship breaks down, you are forced to spend time in isolation or experience periods of loneliness, you don't have time to exercise—the delicate balance of your ANS can become disrupted: dysregulated.

Your nervous system is unique to you, which means that how your body and brain express disruptions or issues within your nervous system is going to be completely individual.

Nervous system dysregulation can manifest in a broad spectrum of symptoms from an annoying headache, all the way through to life-threatening seizures.

Some common symptoms of nervous system dysregulation are:

- over- or underreacting
- sensory sensitivity
- exhaustion
- memory problems
- digestive issues
- difficulty relaxing
- allergies or intolerances
- headaches and/or migraines
- sweating
- dizziness/vertigo
- nausea
- insomnia (difficulty falling or staying asleep)
- restlessness
- irritability

Nervous system dysregulation means that your body and mind are in a constant state of survival. This may look like being on edge or on high alert, or being triggered easily—you're perceiving threat or danger when there isn't necessarily an actual threat in front of you.

Your nervous system learns through experience, which means that throughout your life you have collected certain experiences that your nervous system integrates and learns to be "threatening." This may manifest as fight, flight or freeze responses (see pages 33–36), which can interfere with day-to-day life and relationships.

As you can imagine, if you're in a state of dysregulation, it's not conducive to you thinking—or even dreaming—big. Everything that comes your way will be treated like an intruder. This leads to huge emotions, scary thoughts and overwhelming feelings that may not necessarily match up to the stimulus that you are dealing with. A dysregulated nervous system will either overreact or underreact to stimuli. The root cause is usually linked to an unresolved or unfinished stress response from your past.

When someone experiences dysregulation, it can be a sign that they are suffering from an imbalanced ANS. These symptoms can be so severe that they are debilitating, making it difficult for individuals to function in their daily lives.

WHAT IMPACTS THE NERVOUS SYSTEM?

Everything in your life—from the foods you eat and the amount of sleep you get to your exercise habits, and everything else in between—influences your physiology and how it functions.

Below we'll explore a few of these, such as dysfunctional breathing patterns, environmental toxins, lack of sleep and processed foods, and how they can impact the nervous system causing dysregulation.

Dysfunctional breathing patterns

It is estimated that over 60 percent of those who experience anxiety also have breathing-pattern disorders. This means that they are breathing too fast, too shallowly, too much and often into their chest rather than their diaphragm, which keeps their sympathetic nervous system switched on all the time.

If you've ever had the opportunity to watch a baby breathing, you may have noticed that their belly expands and contracts when they breathe in and out. Babies naturally breathe using their diaphragms, which causes their bellies—and often the rest of their bodies—to rise and fall along with each inhalation and exhalation.

Breathing into our bellies is a skill that we all possess at birth but have usually lost by the time we're adults. This can be due to a number of factors—trauma, chronic stress, anxiety, asthma, infections and illnesses, to name a few. Regardless of the cause, chronic incorrect and inefficient breathing patterns that become normalized throughout our lifetime cause the nerve that controls the diaphragm (the phrenic nerve) to "forget" how to breathe correctly. In other words, instead of breathing into the diaphragm (belly breathing), we breathe high in the chest (chest breathing).

The diaphragm contracts rhythmically and continually as we breathe. It's responsible for most of the breathing process, even though it usually happens without our conscious effort. When you inhale, the diaphragm contracts and flattens. This makes more room for your lungs to fill with air. When you exhale, the diaphragm relaxes and returns to its domelike shape. Air is forced out of your lungs as a result.

By not engaging the diaphragm, the lungs do not create a vacuum effect, which in turn prevents the lungs from expanding to their full potential. When the lungs don't expand fully, they don't activate the vagus nerve, which leads to less efficient vagus nerve signaling, thus lowering the vagal tone in a person.

Incorrect breathing patterns cause a decrease in lung capacity, inflammation and oxidative stress (see page 59). This can lead to a host of problems including anxiety, panic attacks, lower back pain, chest infections and fatigue. A dysfunctional breathing pattern can also cause neck and shoulder pain, headaches, migraines and much more. We will address what you can do to improve your breathing patterns in the Reset Program in Part 2.

Gut health and bacterial overgrowth

The gut–brain connection is one of the most fascinating and under-explored areas of neuroscience, and there is still so much to learn about how our gut microbiota, hormones and neurotransmitters impact our mental health.

You may have heard your gut referred to as your "second brain" and that's because this complex system consists of over 100 million neurons lining your gut walls. Information is sent predominantly from the gut to the brain through the vagus nerve. This bidirectional highway of communication between the brain and gut offers a vital transportation route for neu-rotransmitters, like serotonin. About 95 percent of the hormone serotonin, which regulates emotions and moods, is made in the gut.

For the relationships between the vagus nerve, gut and brain to flourish, they need to be, in a sense, "happy" and healthy. They achieve this happy and healthy relationship through staying in constant communication with one another—like sending a check-in message to your best friend.

In the same way that you share what's going on in your life with your best friend—the good, the bad and the ugly—so too do the gut, vagus nerve and brain. If something goes wrong and one of them isn't feeling great or is not functioning optimally, then it impacts the other organs and systems in this relation-ship, and they also start to feel a bit "off." The same is true in reverse: if one is super happy and feeling fantastic, this flows over to the others in the relationship too!

A clear example of this relationship in real life is the experience of having butterflies in your stomach. If you're feeling excited or nervous, the gut reflects the same feelings and behaviors. Similarly, if you get food poisoning and consequently your gut is not in the best shape, then you may notice that your brain also feels slow and foggy, and you may find it difficult to see the positive in life in that moment.

The ecosystem that lives within your gut is called the micro-biome and is crucial for our health, but also extremely delicate. One small change can affect the whole ecosystem. In your gut microbiome, there are trillions of bacteria, microbes, fungi and viruses that help you digest your food, protect you against harmful pathogens and even regulate your immune system. The balance between all of these different bacteria and microbes in your gut can change over time depending on what you eat. For example, eating a Western diet high in processed foods and sugars can change your gut microbiota by promoting growth of unhealthy bacteria, such as E. coli. The composition of your gut microbiome can also be influenced by environmental factors such as stress, pollution and antibiotics. As we age, our microbiomes change in response to these factors.

In the groundbreaking SMILES Trial, researchers demonstrated how nutrition has a significant impact on our mood. The 12-week-long study examined how a modified Mediterranean diet—which consists of 40 percent carbohydrate, 30 percent protein and the remaining 30 percent fat—affects depression symptoms. The study showed that people in the dietary intervention group experienced a greater reduction in their symptoms of depression over three months compared to those who were simply given social support. Among those receiving dietary support, a third of the participants met criteria for remission of major depression at the end of the trial; among those receiving social support only, just 8 percent went into remission.

The impressive remission rate among those receiving dietary support in the study highlights the critical role that a balanced gut microbiome plays in improving mental health outcomes like depression.

When the balance within your gut microbiome tips too far in the way of bad bacteria, it can lead to something called oxidative stress, which can damage cells, proteins and DNA in the body, as well as damaging the vagus nerve.

Bacterial overgrowth in the gut not only causes the brain to reflect and mirror the same experiences as the gut, but it also causes a disruption in the communication between the gut and the brain. When these two organs don't communicate well, they aren't able to make good decisions or help one another effectively, which leads to further issues in both the brain and body.

Processed foods

Several studies have found that foods containing emulsifiers and preservatives—designed to achieve shelf-life extension— are linked to increased levels of inflammation and changes in the gut microbiome, leaning towards dysbiosis (the technical term for an imbalance of the microorganisms, mainly bacteria, which live in the intestines and make up the gut flora, or microbiome).

Recent research has shown that food that is rich in saturated or trans-fatty acids activates inflammatory markers within the gut and in the body when consumed in large quantities.

The nutrition of the entire body plays a crucial role in the production of neurotransmitters in the brain as well. In the absence of sufficient proteins, minerals, vitamins and other nutrient sources in a diet, an individual may have difficulty forming an appropriate balance of neurotransmitters.

Stress

There is good stress and bad stress in our lives. It seems that we especially need to experience some good stress. Also known as "eustress," good stress is the kind of stress that helps us grow and feel our best.

Among some of the most common types of "eustress" that people experience are working out at the gym; traveling to a new country to experience its culture and architecture; having a baby and helping it to develop into a healthy, happy adult; and beginning a new relationship and the stressors that come with it.

In contrast to this, as we've seen, long-term, chronic stress can cause fight-or-flight, or shutdown (see pages 33–36). There is an increase in adrenaline and norepinephrine. Norepinephrine is a hormone and neurotransmitter that regulates heart rate, blood pressure, temperature control and arousal. It also plays a role in the body's response to stress levels as a result of this, leading to a decrease in acetylcholine levels. Acetylcholine is a neurotransmitter that plays a crucial role in memory, learning, attention, arousal and involuntary muscle movement.

Lack of sleep

We often underestimate the power of sleep: there can be serious consequences when we don't get enough of it.

A good night's sleep is crucial to restoring and rebuilding tissues in the body, repairing damaged cells, eliminating toxins, releasing hormones and manufacturing new proteins.

For your brain to function properly, you must have access to adequate sleep. Not getting enough sleep or being tired disrupts genes that are responsible for regulating your circadian rhythm, which greatly reduces your ability to complete tasks and regulate your emotions.

Lack of sleep can also have a detrimental effect on your memory, as tiredness reduces activity within your hippocampus, which is the brain's memory center.

Losing even a few hours has a negative effect on your executive functioning, reducing your capacity to concentrate and pay attention as well as lowering your threshold for reasoning and problem-solving. We will look at ways that you can improve your sleep in the Reset Program in Part 2.

Alcohol and substances

Alcohol has the ability to cross the blood–brain barrier, which can be thought of as a protective layer of the central nervous system that stops harmful toxins and/or pathogens that could cause infections from entering the brain.

Because of the ease with which alcohol can cross the blood–brain barrier, it has the capacity to reach different areas of the body relatively quickly. In the brain, alcohol's effects are far-reaching. Generally, alcohol is a depressant on the central nervous system, slowing down physiological processes, resulting in feeling calm, sleepy or less inhibited.

Alcohol has some pretty serious negative effects on the brain: it causes brain tissue to contract (shrink), kills brain cells and—over prolonged periods of time—can seriously impact cognitive and memory abilities and capacity.

Environmental toxins

Environmental toxins are an unfortunate, inescapable part of life in the twenty-first century. They come at you from things like pesticides and herbicides, hormone-disrupting compounds found in plastics like phthalates and BPA, heavy metals, air and noise pollution, cigarette smoke and vapes, ultra-processed foods, fragrance and even some prescribed medications.

Recent studies found a troubling 200 chemicals present in newborn umbilical cord blood.

As chemicals are not adequately labeled or passed through testing for safety, these toxins have a free pass to wreak havoc on our nervous system. They can impact cognitive and neurological function, fertility and reproductive function, trigger weight changes and autoimmune conditions such as eczema and alter blood glucose balance.

Dysregulation is essentially an imbalance between the branches of the nervous system—usually when the fight-or-flight or freeze states become more dominant and the ventral vagal system gets harder to access in order to rest and relax.

In modern society, it's not hard to see dysregulation manifest itself everywhere. From the stressful commute in peak-hour traffic, to the environmental toxins we are constantly exposed to, your brain and body are in a constant battle. When the body is in a constant state of survival, it wears you down. Nervous system regulation is an ongoing process of noticing when you are in a state of arousal or hypoarousal, and having the tools and resources to either downregulate (if you're in fight-or-flight) or upregulate (if you're in dorsal vagal) in order to bring your entire nervous system back to a state of safety within your ventral vagal nervous system.

Without being consciously aware of our own lifestyle practices and environment, our nervous system can become impacted and dysregulated. In Part 2, we will begin to look at a number of functional and effective lifestyle changes that can help you to create an environment that is supportive of your nervous system.

The more that you hone the skills outlined in the Reset Program, the more resilient your nervous system will become. You'll start to notice that, even when you're feeling triggered, maybe the reaction isn't as big or dramatic as it once was. And this is because you are teaching your body and mind to trust in your ability to gently guide yourself back to a calm and grounded state.

4.
TUNING INTO YOUR BODY

By 18 years old I felt untethered. Every part of my body and mind felt foreign to me, like I was sleepwalking through life. I felt like a shapeshifter. I could switch on a smile and add some charm when I needed to in order to get through public situations, but would then return home and crumble into a heap.

I had always loved sports, but as I grew older, I forgot how formidable I felt when I moved my body in functional ways and I stopped. Until one day, when I was driving down a road that went past a mixed martial arts gym.

Many a time I had driven past and felt a longing to go in, but I'd always been too fearful to even set foot inside the place. For whatever reason, on this day I decided to quickly pull over. This was it—I was going to go in. I sat in the car for about 20 minutes, planning out all of my escape routes if, for some reason, things went terribly wrong. I took a deep breath, got out of my car and walked through the doors of the gym.

I stood awkwardly in front of the receptionist, saying yes to signing up for a trial class the following day. Every alarm bell in my body was screaming, *Get the hell out of here, you don't belong*, but I was stoic in my decision for once. I had listened to those unhelpful voices in my head for so long and, although I had never been more disconnected and in pain than I was in that moment, I knew something had to change.

The next day I arrived and was sweating bullets before the class even began. I was the only female there and I felt extremely uncomfortable. I barely made it through the warm-up—my whole body was tingling and struggling for air—but then the pad work started and I threw a punch for the first time since I was six years old in a taekwondo lesson.

Something about the movement flicked a switch in my brain. It felt good. Like, really good. Was I good at it? Definitely not. But my body responded in a way that was similar to a sigh of relief. My muscles tensed and relaxed; the lactic acid built up; and the impact reverberated from my fist, all the way to my toes.

It was the first time I had connected with my body in many years, and it was the first time I had experienced my body respond with a resounding "yes" for almost a decade.

Exhausted, red-faced and spent, I finished the class and had a calmness and clarity in my mind that almost scared me. I didn't have any money, so I used what I had on my credit card to buy a set of gloves and pay for a month of training, and I would figure out the rest along the way.

All I knew was that through sheer coincidence, I had found something that drastically changed my state of mind, my emotional state and the way in which I perceived the world around me. I wanted to understand why and how something so simple could make a bigger impact on my mental health than the ten years of therapy I had done. The curiosity that was kindled within me that day was the beautiful catalyst that led me to enroll in university and begin studying psychology.

This was my first step in reclamation. I *felt* for the first time in a long while and I knew that this was something that I simply had to do; it wasn't a choice.

RECLAIMING YOUR BODY AND MIND

RECLAMATION (NOUN): THE PROCESS OF CLAIMING SOMETHING BACK OR OF REASSERTING A RIGHT

Do you need to go and start combat sports in order to reclaim your body and mind? No—it's definitely not for everyone! What my story demonstrates, though, is how reclamation starts with a reconnection to the body—to *feeling* the body once again.

This process of noticing, embracing and understanding the sensations that visit your body is a journey that can take time. Similar to starting a new relationship, where we explore and hold space for another person, hoping to catch a glimpse or insight into their true feelings, we must rekindle and nurture the relationship that we have with our body. That involves carefully exploring the parts of us that may feel safe or even good. Building affinity with your body takes time and curiosity, and, with attention, we begin to tune into the subtle cues and non-verbal language of our internal world.

When you are in a state of being chronically disconnected from yourself, it has some pretty major impacts on not only your mental health, but also your physical health and relationships. The feeling of loneliness and isolation becomes ever-present: even when you are surrounded by others, there's that awful sensation in the pit of your stomach that never seems to go away.

This growing distance between your mind and body only exacerbates already overwhelming mental health issues, keeping you trapped in patterns of self-defeating behaviors and thoughts.

We no longer see ourselves as who we truly are, so the seemingly "simple" acts of looking after ourselves—like drinking enough water every day and eating healthy foods to nourish our body—slip away. These may seem like small things, but over months and years, something like chronic dehydration and lack of nutrients from your diet can lead to significant physical health issues, such as high blood pressure, cardiovascular disease and immune system dysfunction.

Disconnection in relationships can lead to a breakdown of communication and intimacy, which in turn causes feelings of estrangement and separation from loved ones. It can also contribute to the breakdown of social networks, which are often crucial sources of psychological and physiological support during difficult times.

When we are disconnected from ourselves, we have a harder time making decisions, knowing and aligning with our own values, voicing our needs and taking action on our goals. We begin to feel uncertain in our ability to navigate the world and lose trust in ourselves.

Reclamation can encompass everything from physical possessions to aspects of your identity. In the context of this book, reclamation is a radical act of reclaiming parts of yourself that you have lost touch with or that have been taken from you. Without your natural confidence, you may have shrunk yourself down, lost the spark of creativity or, maybe, you feel like you've lost your sense of purpose in life. Reclamation is also the beautiful process of rediscovering your sense of power and agency where once you may have felt powerless, helpless or lost.

Reclamation is a radical act because, in a world where we may feel like we are "less than," "not enough" or "broken," we take back our power and ownership over all parts of ourselves, our healing journeys and all that is important to us, regardless of our history or past experiences.

Self-trust is a fundamental tenet of personal growth and development, and plays an important role in rebuilding connection. A lack of self-trust erodes your confidence in social situations and eats away at your relationships, leaving you feeling insecure and fearful of abandonment and rejection.

In the journey of reconnection and reclamation, there needs to be a strong foundation of self-trust. This involves developing a deep understanding of our values, needs and goals, and learning to navigate and trust our own judgment and intuition.

In Part 2, we will explore a range of techniques that will support you in rekindling a deep connection with both your body and mind and forging a strong sense of self-trust. But first we need to understand why this connection to your body is so powerful, and how your body plays a role in the expression of your mental health.

UNDERSTANDING THE MIND-BODY CONNECTION

Have you ever been so nervous that your hands started to shake? Maybe you've felt so scared that you felt frozen in time. Or maybe you've found yourself lying in bed at night unable to sleep because you're worried about something.

Your emotions impact your body and the various physical sensations you have. They also change your behaviors and impact your natural physiological processes.

We feel emotional pain deep within our body. If you've ever gone through a bad break-up or grieved someone you've lost, you may have felt "heartache." If you were excited for an upcoming event or feeling nervous about something, you may have felt "butterflies" in your stomach.

The mind and the body are intricately connected through complex systems to create a powerful and formidable human experience. This connection brings you together as a whole. Your brain is not separate from your body as we may have once believed. The mind–body connection is the link that creates you—your thoughts, behaviors, attitudes and beliefs—and ultimately determines how you live your life, the decisions you make and your physical health.

The science behind the mind-body connection

What's the first thing you think of when you hear the word "connection?" Maybe it's a cable that needs to be plugged in or an electrical current passing through two points. Whatever your answer, there's probably a very good chance it's not quite as warm and fuzzy as the idea of connecting with yourself.

But here's the thing—your body is your best friend, and your mind is like its partner in crime. They're both working together to help keep you alive, happy and healthy—and when they're not working together? You may as well be running around in circles desperately trying to find a place to plug in your phone or laptop.

The mind and body are connected in more ways than one: our psychological states have physical consequences, and our physical states have psychological consequences. They can also affect our health and expression of ill health or disease. Since our minds and bodies are always talking to each other (even if we don't always listen), the connection between them is critical for maintaining good health overall.

To better understand this connection and how it affects our behavior, feelings and emotions, we need to understand the different ways in which the mind and body are connected.

Brains are amazing and complex organs; they are often called the "body's command centers" or "human supercomputers." But the brain is more than just a machine—it is deeply integrated into the rest of the body.

Although we do not yet fully understand how mind–body communication occurs, scientists are discovering some ways to improve our understanding.

As the "command center," your brain allows you to experience thoughts, beliefs, attitudes and emotions. This is what you would refer to as your "mind."

Hormones and neurotransmitters, which act as chemical

and physical messengers, facilitate communication within the brain but also throughout the brain and the body.

Stress, anxiety and depression, as well as other mental states, can affect how well—or not so well—your organs function.

There is increasing scientific evidence that hormones and neurotransmitters that are associated with emotion can also affect our bodies physically, shifting our blood pressure, heart rate, sleep patterns, appetite and sleep quality.

This connection between the mind and body is beautifully illustrated in a medical trial undertaken by David Spiegel, Director of Stanford University's Psychosocial Research Laboratory, who found that women with breast cancer who participated in group mindfulness therapy lived longer, had less pain and had a higher quality of life.

Further research has also determined that stress reduces our body's ability to fight off infection, illness and disease by altering blood cell function. Increasing stress results in a decreased immune response from white blood cells, infected cells and cancerous cells. What's more, studies on individuals with anxiety and depression found increased inflammatory markers that reduced the ability of the body to heal wounds.

Understanding and honoring this important holistic view of your mind and body as one gives you back the capacity to integrate all parts of yourself. It gives you the keys to the "root cause" of issues, rather than just looking at the symptoms or manifestations and putting a Band-Aid over them.

This holistic philosophy is not a new theory or idea: it has been around for many thousands of years throughout many cultures. As Western thought struggled with the idea of mind–

body connection, Buddhist philosophy and Eastern traditions such as Ayurveda (whose lineage can be traced to Vedic systems in India) stressed the interaction between them.

Leaning back into this ancient philosophy of the mind–body connection has been a gradual wave you may have noticed occurring in Western society. We are beginning to not only see the importance of this connection, we are also starting to reclaim it: your relationship to your body and, in turn, wholeness.

THE CHANGING FACE OF MENTAL HEALTH CARE

If you think back to times throughout your life when you were experiencing emotions such as fear, anxiety, grief or depression, can you remember what or who it was that helped you feel better in those moments?

For me, through the dark moments, it wasn't often that I felt truly supported by words alone. For example, when I was experiencing the dark heavy weight of depression, often the most powerful thing was simply being in the company of someone I felt safe with. Words didn't even have to pass their lips—just being in their presence was comforting.

It was the same in moments of high anxiety or panic. I found that touch was a strongly grounding and calming resource. An enfolding hug, a containment—something that felt as though it held me within defined walls. A gesture that felt real and safe and brought me back into the ventral vagal state of connection.

In grief, what gave me solace were those people or things in life that allowed me space to safely express my emotions. Then, deeply convulsing tears would course through my body when I reminisced or looked at something that reminded me of what or who had been lost.

It was the ecstatic movement that shifted the very core of my physiological experience from one state into a sometimes momentary feeling of simply something else—a surprising but invaluable discovery.

The common theme throughout all of these powerful experiences was that words were not present. Words don't serve your internal experience justice when you feel like you're no longer in control of your experience.

Yet although as a society we are becoming more open and compassionate in our approach to mental health issues, the narrative we hear is pretty much always: *You just have to talk about it.*

Talk therapy: a Band-Aid, not a solution

Mental health care comes in many shapes and sizes, with talk therapy providing a safe space for individuals to express and work through their emotions and experiences without fear of judgment.

Talk therapy has the capacity to explore thought patterns and behaviors and examine how they may be impacting mental health. For example, it can help individuals to better understand how their thoughts and beliefs about themselves and the world influence their emotional responses or behavior. However, there are drawbacks to this approach. It is often too general and does not take into account an individual's unique traits and circumstances.

This is partly due to standardization of mental health care practices—the implementation of *The Diagnostic and Statistical Manual of Mental Disorders* (*DSM*), for example—which can negate or eliminate important cultural nuances when it comes to evaluating clients' experiences. The *DSM* provides a set of criteria to help practitioners diagnose mental health disorders, but it is often criticized for being too general and not taking into account the individual differences between clients. For instance, a doctor may diagnose someone with depression based on their symptoms alone, without taking into account the context or root causes of these symptoms.

Additionally, talk therapy can take a long time to provide results. This is especially true for people who may have experienced trauma or have many issues that need to be addressed before they feel comfortable enough to express themselves.

Individuals who have experienced trauma, anxiety and ongoing stress may find it challenging to connect with their emotions on a truly restorative level. Instead of feeling the actual experience, they may try to understand the emotional experience by intellectualizing it—by talking about it or writing down what happened, which has long been the prevailing approach in society. Intellectualizing those emotions acts as a protective defense mechanism as words can often block access to emotions, which are felt in the limbic system of the brain. When we cannot access our emotions we feel disconnected from ourselves and others. The ability to connect with our emotions is what helps us feel connected to the world around us.

A question you may need to ask yourself is, what are you trying to achieve when you use your mind to solve your emotional pain? Subconsciously, the true goal is often to avoid feeling the pain altogether, while simultaneously feeling as though we are doing something about it. One of the most effective ways to achieve this is by coming up with many different problems and "solutions."

This was true in my case—I found myself on a never-ending merry-go-round of identifying what I believed to be the "problem." Anything from stress about schoolwork, teenage boyfriends and playground drama, to my parents and teachers not "getting it," people watching television or talking overly loudly, or being told I couldn't do certain things—all of these external problems needed to be solved and then I would, or so I believed, feel better, or at least different. Unfortunately, the more I tried to solve and remove these issues from my life, the more problems seemed to appear and the worse I felt.

These solutions help us feel as though we are "doing the work"; they alleviate the difficult emotions of fear, anger, loneliness and grief for a moment. But in the long run, can you really think of a solution for experiencing loss and grief? Can you find a solution to that feeling of burning anger caused by a great hurt you suffered? Can you "solve" the experience of anxiety or depression, or chronic, ongoing stress?

If you are able to intellectualize and verbalize your experience, are you accessing the core of the emotion itself and moving towards healing? Or do you learn to become adept at retelling a story about yourself? In other words, are you able to successfully quieten the loud, intellectual part of the brain that is trying to protect you enough to hear, feel and connect with the parts of your brain, body and nervous system that have not had the opportunity to successfully process and finish the stress response cycle from that experience?

If when you first seek help, you find your emotions dominating and spilling over when prompted to talk about emotional experiences, what then? Chances are you begin forming a protective emotional barrier that stops you from getting close to the original emotional wound and feeling the pain associated with it. This too impedes your ability to access and process (identify, feel the emotion of and then integrate) the experience in any restorative or healing way.

The human mind will always work to protect you from anything that it believes to be too painful. While well-intentioned, this often leads to further pain, emotional suffering and frustration when attempts to solve the problem fall short.

Talking about emotional experiences and using expressive language is a beautiful and necessary part of the healing process—but it's only one piece of the puzzle. As a standalone form of therapeutic treatment, it does not have the depth and capacity to successfully attend to emotional pain in a way that allows for an experience to be safely processed and released. Words can only take you so far in your understanding and pro-cessing of your experiences.

Luckily, with the rise of the digital age, the field of mental health is beginning to see more diversity and a development of new scientific theories and practices. As many people seek holistic approaches to their mental health care, alternatives to traditional talk therapy are gaining traction.

In order to access the benefits of talk therapy, perhaps it is better to start your healing journey by first addressing trapped, painful emotions by this new means—starting with the body. To truly "heal" and change your patterns, you need to go deeper and into the somatic.

Somatic therapy

Somatic therapy—an umbrella term for body-centred techniques— takes into account the mind and body's interrelatedness and recognizes the importance of the body in healing emotional trauma and promoting overall wellness.

Wilhelm Reich, an Austrian psychoanalyst who lived from 1897 to 1957, is believed to have made the largest impact on the early development and establishment of somatic psychotherapy as a therapeutic model. Its basis is that our bodies hold pain and trauma in muscle tension and fascia (connective tissues). Somatic therapy is a powerful approach that uses the body as a tool to understand and heal emotional trauma. Somatic therapy also focuses on the relationship between mind, body and emotion. It holds that emotions are directly related to our physical sensations—a person who is feeling anxious about something might have butterflies in their tummy or feel like they have heartburn, for example.

There are many different techniques used in somatic therapy, but some of the most common include body awareness, movement and touch. Body awareness involves helping individuals become more aware of their bodily sensations and emotions, while movement and touch are used to release physical tension and promote emotional healing. For example, a somatic therapist may use movement techniques such as yoga or dance to help release physical tension and enable their client to connect with their emotions. Touch techniques such as massage or acupressure may also be used to aid the release of tension and promote relaxation.

Somatic therapy focuses on how we experience ourselves in relation to the world around us, what our feeling responses are towards others—and even how those feelings have been conditioned by previous trauma.

Both polyvagal theory and the different somatic therapies recognize the importance of the mind–body connection and the impact that emotional trauma can have on physical health. By addressing the physical, emotional and cognitive aspects of trauma, these therapies can provide individuals with a comprehensive approach to healing.

Somatic therapy and polyvagal theory are ushering in a new age of mental health care that truly recognizes the individual as a whole, with all their experiences, using a "bottom-up" approach to overcoming issues such as anxiety, trauma and stress. "Bottom-up" approaches are not new—they inform age-old well-being practices such as yoga, for example—but they are making a comeback to the mental health arsenal and are also vastly different to the conventional top-down approach, which most traditional talk therapies follow.

Academically paraphrased, it goes like this:

Cognition, or the process of thinking, utilizes top-down processing and occurs within the prefrontal cortex (PFC) region of the brain. It looks at how we interpret information and use it to change our thought patterns—in other words, this approach tries to influence behavior by changing what people think about things. Cognitive methods, such as cognitive behavioral therapy (CBT), rely on your ability to be aware of what you think and then consciously change those thoughts.

Bottom-up approaches begin with the body and its sensations and movements. It views the input of sensory information from the external and internal environments as providing a basis for how your body lets your brain know whether it is safe or not. These processes occur unconsciously, meaning they are not influenced by the PFC. The bottom-up approach teaches us about the wisdom of our body and how movement can unlock emotions held in our fascia. Because trauma can be difficult to recall or remember, bottom-up approaches use the body rather than the mind to access and process traumatic experiences.

Somatic therapies and polyvagal theory work primarily using bottom-up processing at the start of an individual's healing journey—that is, accessing emotions by considering physiological responses. Once an individual's body has been attended to, they can then access cognitive processes in a more meaningful capacity, so these techniques integrate top-down processing as well—tackling issues from both directions.

Through somatic therapy, you can learn to release physical tension, regulate your emotions and develop a greater sense of safety and self-awareness. The Reset Program in Part 2 draws on somatic therapies and polyvagal theory in order to create an integrative and holistic approach to help you heal and overcome anxiety, post-traumatic stress, chronic stress and trauma.

Working with the body to reclaim safety

"The body keeps the score" is a phrase popularized by renowned psychiatrist and trauma expert Bessel van der Kolk; it's also the title of his bestselling book. Essentially, what it means is that your body holds on to past experiences in order to protect you today.

When you work with the body, you bypass your cognition and, instead of analyzing your experiences, connect with yourself from a place of instinct and bodily wisdom.

Because our minds are so powerful, they close off certain aspects of painful experiences and parts of ourselves that might be too overwhelming or difficult for us to handle on our own. For example, you might be able to talk through your problems with friends or go on a trip and have fun, but no amount of these distractions will give you that sense of inner peace unless the body is attended to—because it's only accessing one small part of the bigger root cause or tension that created the problem in the first place.

In Chapter 6 you will learn two techniques—breathwork and movement—which can help change the brain, ANS and vagus nerve to become less hypervigilant, anxious or stressed.

Once you feel safe and secure, you may be able to revisit past experiences that triggered your body's survival responses. When you feel safe within your body, you expand your capacity to remain present and grounded when you're processing past experiences. You have an anchor in the present moment that you know you can return to any time you are feeling overwhelmed or distressed.

Working with the body to release trauma doesn't require an understanding or explanation of why you're experiencing it—the act of releasing trauma can be accomplished without knowing where it came from.

RECLAIMING YOUR BODY WITH SOMATICS

After leaving the hospital following the roller coaster accident in 2003, I was ready to jump back into being a kid, but my body had other plans. Not only did I have a bruised heart, which meant that my heart rate was constantly elevated, but I also began experiencing something that I had never felt before.

Whenever I would watch a movie or TV show that showed a high-pace car chase or accident, or even when I was in the car myself with my family, driving at normal speeds, my body would respond with this intense and visceral reaction of fear. My heart rate would hit the high 200bpms, I would feel all my muscles tense and brace for potential impact and my mind would be running wild with all the potential catastrophic outcomes that it could conjure.

Trauma is a relatively misunderstood term, and I definitely didn't understand at ten years old that what I was experiencing was a trauma response. That's because I had learned that trauma was something that only occurred in events like war, brutal assaults or abuse, or catastrophic natural disasters. Only as an adult did I begin to unfurl and uncover the true depths of trauma and the subsequent and diverse reactions that it can create within the human body and mind.

In Chapter 2 I talked about the recent developments in our understanding of trauma. Traumatic events can be anything in life that come at you too fast, too soon or are too much for your brain, body and nervous system to handle in that moment. While there are certain events that are undoubtedly inherently traumatic—the sorts of things listed in the previous paragraph—trauma is far less about the event itself than was previously thought. We now know that trauma is not necessarily held in the event, but more so in how the individual responds to the event. There's also a much more nuanced and broad experience of trauma—for example, a child who grows up in a household where there are daily displays of frightening anger may go through life carrying symptoms of trauma. It is recognized that this occurs more than we once imagined.

In my case, at the age of ten, I had no idea that the dream-like state I was experiencing was actually a state of dorsal vagal (see page 20) dissociation. My body and brain were smart enough to realize that the pain of what I was experiencing was too much for me to handle in that moment, so I drifted into a sort of out-of-body experience, in which, for a long time, I felt nothing—a sense of numbness—about the event itself.

My subsequent reactions were to pretend as though nothing had even happened—to brush it off, to try to return to who I was as a ten-year-old. But try as I might, I felt like I had lost my way; I couldn't find the same carefree, happy kid I was before.

On a more subtle end of the spectrum, trauma can be experienced through events like not being shown the love and attention you deserve, experiencing bullying or going through an intense break-up.

Anything that happens to you over the course of your life can be potentially traumatic, depending on the state you are in. What I mean by that is children often experience these more subtle events of trauma such as lack of attention, and it is potentially traumatic because, as a child, your whole world depends on having someone to nurture and look after you.

It's too much for your body and mind to handle, but your body and mind are also adaptive. You might learn to look after yourself, have a make-believe friend or look for love and attention in other creative ways.

As an adult, if someone ignores you, you are probably more equipped to handle the experience, so it may not leave such a lasting impact on you. But as an adult, the pressures that you experience are different. Trying to handle financial pressures, job demands and then on top of that going through a break-down of a relationship may simply be too much for you to juggle at that point in time.

Trauma can be big events, but it can also be many small cuts that occur over a period of time, chipping away at you.

Traumatic events can cause your body to go into survival mode, in which the heart beats faster and blood pressure rises while digestion slows down. This reaction is meant to help you survive stressful situations by making sure that the organs essential for fighting or running away from danger are able to function properly.

The brain goes into an "emergency mode" when you experience trauma—allowing it to focus on immediate life-or-death issues. This can cause a glitch in your body's memory-processing system, leaving traumatic events unprocessed by both the mind and body.

As we explored earlier, treatment for trauma typically involves the use of psychotherapy and/or pharmaceuticals. Although this approach can be useful for many trauma survivors, it does not address the fundamental issue of how we hold on to and adapt to traumatic events within our bodies. Nor does this approach take into account that mental, physical and emotional processes are related.

Trauma keeps the mind and body in a state of high alert, as if danger is imminent. This can manifest itself physically by causing symptoms such as hypertension, shallow breathing, muscle tension and pain. It's common to experience chronic muscle tension or numbness, which can lead to spasms, fibromyalgia, migraines and other types of pain.

Emerging evidence suggests that trauma doesn't only affect your brain—it can influence your cells too. Recent studies reveal that stem cells can actually store memories of past events, and these "issues in your tissues" may be harming both physical and emotional health. Trauma that is not processed can lead to health problems such as heart attack, stroke, obesity and diabetes.

If trauma or "trapped" emotions are ignored for long enough, they may be manifested as physical sensations, such as chronic pain. However, releasing those trapped emotions, sensations and experiences can have equally dramatic positive effects on our well-being and physical health.

Somatic release practices can be effective because they address the same physiological response to stress that all mammals share. If you have ever been startled, it is likely that your body reacted by shaking or trembling. This natural response occurs when our bodies release an immediate rush of adrenaline during times of high stress (processing threats and releasing stress hormones).

For various reasons, in humans, the body's natural sequence may be interrupted. In some cases, we actively stop the sequence. When we feel scared, anxious or stressed, maybe we learn to hide our natural desires and instincts, to put on a mask and march on through the storm that is happening beneath the surface. We may find ways to hide our shaking, trembling or desire to get away because we feel ashamed. Alternatively, we may become distracted—immersed in gaming or social media, for instance—or disconnected from our emotions, and this too may interfere with the body's natural responses. The consequence is that we may carry in our bodies these incomplete stress response cycles, which block us from returning to baseline.

The somatic release practices that we'll explore in the Reset Program address these unfinished stress response cycles. They help us expend or allow that energy that is bubbling under the surface to come up and out—how nature intended it to.

Coming back to the fact that all mammals have a stress response cycle, think about the severe stressors that are a daily part of a wild animal's life. By allowing for their natural cycle, such as shaking or trembling, they are able to rebound quickly and resume their normal patterns of behavior. That is the aim of somatic release practices.

At its core, the mind–body connection is the interrelationship between an individual's mental and physical health. It refers to how emotional well-being can affect your physical health—and vice versa.

We see this complex connection play out in real life when, for example, you may experience anxiety coupled with physical symptoms such as headaches, fatigue and digestive issues. Similarly, chronic physical health conditions, like chronic pain or illness, can affect mental well-being negatively.

What does this mean for you? If you're often confused by what's going on in your body, this is your first prompt to begin *listening*. Your body is always talking to you—it has needs, desires and feelings that aren't always obvious. If you're not listening closely enough, then it may be easy to miss what your body is trying to tell you. In the Reset Program in Part 2, you will learn how to tune into those messages.

In a society where fitting in often feels safer than being authentic (which we discuss in greater detail in Chapter 6), it is a radical act to reclaim all parts of yourself as being worthy. It is also a radical act to accept yourself completely and entirely without condition.

This may feel like the most difficult thing you'll ever do. It will challenge everything you believe about yourself, your value and importance in this world.

It will also be one of the most rewarding experiences of your life. As you begin to forge a strong connection between your body and mind, you will start to gently weave all parts of yourself back into a state of wholeness.

Now, let's delve into Part 2, where we explore how you can foster trust, safety and connection in order to radically transform and heal your life.

PART 2

THE VAGUS NERVE RESET

5.
ABOUT THE VAGUS NERVE RESET PROGRAM

In the Vagus Nerve Reset Program, there are three phases to harnessing your body's natural ability to restore balance. These phases are designed to heal trauma, anxiety and stress one step at a time—first by reclaiming your sense of safety, then learning how to reconnect with your body and finally applying these techniques in real-life situations.

Healing does not have a time frame, so do not pressure yourself to rush through and "complete" the phases. This program has been purposely designed without time frames in order for you to work through the phases and resources at your own pace. The program should take as long as you need. You have arrived here at this moment by way of your own experiences, symptoms or desires, and your needs are completely unique to all of those things, which means that you may want to spend more time working through certain phases. You may want to return to particular phases, which I invite you to do. Go back over any or all phases as much as you wish.

No matter where you are starting—whether you have already been through programs, had therapeutic support in the past or this is your very first foray into mental health support—this program can meet you where you're at and hold space for expansion.

Throughout each phase of the program, I will be by your side. From the very first steps where you will create safety and stability, all the way to you blooming confidently in your own body—and taking up space in the world around you.

WHY DO I NEED TO MOVE THROUGH PHASES?

The program is not just theory and education; it's highly practical—designed for you to take action every step of the way. That's why I urge you not to rush through this book, but rather spend time with each phase, practicing what you learn. That way, by the end of the book, you will walk away feeling confident and resilient in your abilities to support your mind and body each and every day. If you go too quickly, you miss the magic that happens when you honor and give space to yourself from a much slower and more conscious perspective.

This is especially true of Phase One. You may have itchy feet and want to speed through it to get to the next phase of processing experiences and emotions, but you would be doing yourself a major disservice if you didn't take your time. Phase One is your foundation, so give yourself a solid base and stay in this phase for as long as you need. No comparing, no competition, just honoring your own timeline.

You will find that each stage of the program builds on what you've already learned, so be sure to complete all of the action steps for each phase before moving on to the next lesson or part of the practice.

Trauma, anxiety and chronic stress can be healed, but not without a firm foundation. Rushing into a space where you are reflecting on past experiences or recurring patterns can bring up many emotions, some of which can disrupt your healing process without the correct resources and tools in place.

When you build out, explore, practice and grasp emotional regulation and self-soothing skills, you move through discomfort and feelings with solid ground under your feet. Moving through each phase allows you to learn, practice and eventually integrate rituals and exercises into your daily life until they become second nature, gradually building up your resilience and capacity to sit with potentially uncomfortable emotions and feelings that might surface.

I won't pretend this is a walk in the park—there is a lot inside these pages. The best approach is to break down each phase by its subheadings. Each subheading can be seen as a "mini-lesson"—at the end of each mini-lesson, reflect on what you have learned. It can be helpful to keep a new notebook and pen by your side to jot down any key takeaways you may have had. Then spend a short period of time implementing any of the exercises or action steps before moving on to your next mini-lesson. Moving through each of the phases in this manner will allow you to explore, experiment and apply what you have learned in a truly conscious and intentional way that will stop you from feeling overwhelmed and allow you to begin experiencing the benefits of your practices straightaway.

With patience and consistency, you'll not only see amazing shifts within, but you'll start to actually feel more and more "like yourself" than you ever have before. Seeing the accumulation of huge shifts in your life will be exciting, rewarding and motivating.

Phase One: Securing your base

During Phase One, the focus is on four areas: establishing a secure base; developing safety and stabilization skills; increasing skill levels; expansion of knowledge.

We'll also set up a hierarchy of needs, which will help you identify what needs to be addressed first and keep you from getting overwhelmed with too much information or too many tasks at once. You'll have the opportunity to practice these skills in real-life situations so that they become second nature to you.

Phase Two: Building body awareness and welcoming in release

In this phase, we shift our focus from working with the external environment to exploring internal experiences. We reconnect you with bodily sensations and movements so that you can better understand how your body functions—what it needs from you and how to give it what it needs.

We will also begin to release held tension in your muscles, joints and connective tissue through emotional release work.

Lastly, we will improve our breathing habits so that we can get balance and regulate our oxygen and carbon dioxide (CO_2) levels for optimal vagal tone and nervous system functioning.

Phase Three: Integrating and nurturing self through connection with others

Finally! I'm going to teach you how to connect with yourself—physically, emotionally and spiritually—so that when you go out into the world again after you've worked your way through this program, you're ready for whatever life brings.

We will begin building strong, mutually supportive relationships through healthy boundaries and clear communication. You'll learn how to reclaim trust in yourself and others, as well as re-establishing trust with your environment. By the end of this phase, you'll be able to leave behind the self-doubts of your past, reigniting your passion for life and opening up a new world of communication possibilities.

HEALING IS NEVER LINEAR; NEITHER ARE THESE PHASES

The process of integrating knowledge, taking action and practicing until it becomes a part of you does not have a set start and finish line. It is dynamic and fluid rather than linear and rigid.

While the phases follow on from one another, you may move from Phase One to Phase Two, only to realize that you indeed have more work that needs to be done in Phase One.

This movement back and forth between the phases is normal

and in fact is encouraged. You may find yourself breezing through certain parts, while others may require more practice, time and attention.

There's no need to push forward when the present moment will illuminate to you whether or not you are ready to proceed to the next page, chapter or phase.

REMEMBERING IS NOT HEALING

When trauma and life experiences have caused a shift in how your mind, body and emotions work together, it can be almost as though the negative event happened yesterday—and you may go around feeling like it could happen again at any moment.

This is your brain doing its job. Because fear is so important to survival, the brain has evolved to rewire itself to be hypervigilant about threats and dangers. At the same time, it tries to avoid situations similar to those that caused the fear in the first place. The part of the brain that monitors basic physiological functions and instinctually reacts to danger (the survival-based "back brain") becomes more active than usual; meanwhile, activity in areas associated with learning and thinking slows down.

But in order to process experiences and emotions, you first need to be able to recognize the underlying emotion. Once that is done, with time and space it can emerge naturally and safely— so you can fully feel it without judgment or without emotions becoming too overwhelming. Part of the processing of emotions is the choice between action or inaction you can take once you have allowed yourself to feel and sit with the emotion. If the emotion is stemming from an issue that is within your control, then there may be an action that you can take to resolve the problem. However, if an emotion is rooted in something beyond your control—such as a traumatic experience or ongoing hardships—you may find it helpful to understand how you can better cope with these situations or learn ways in which to accept and release the experiences.

In order for this process to occur, the back brain, which is associated with emotions and habit responses, must be muted so the reflective front brain can become active.

As we explored in Chapter 4, the belief that "remembering is the way to heal" has dominated the therapeutic landscape since talk therapy was created. With it comes the encouragement to retell and recall traumatic memories, experiences and moments in order to overcome or heal from them. But this push to verbalize and relive often terrifying experiences does not consistently support us in moving forward in our lives. What is often overlooked is how utterly retraumatizing remembering events can be.

Experiences that have impacted our minds and bodies and remain untouched and unprocessed play out in the present moment through our bodily sensations, memories, patterns, responses and flashbacks. While your traumatizing experiences may be logically regarded as "over" and in the past, your body and survival brain continue to dominate the present—forever prepared and playing out the event as if it were happening right here and now. Your survival brain and body don't want to let go of that control as it has been the thing that has helped you survive until this point right now.

In order to regain and reclaim control over your present, you must first be able to show your survival brain and body that you are capable of and safe handling what life throws at you. Learning, implementing and practicing emotional regulation skills—like those included in the Reset Program—until they become as familiar to you as the back of your hand gently guides your brain and body from survival mode into a more open, creative space in which you can learn. The skills, which you practice until they become familiar and safe, now form a secure foundation for you to venture into your past experiences and examine parts of yourself that you have not yet been able to access from a shifted perspective.

In a sense, you create more and more space from experiences until eventually they stop being the dominating narrative that is playing out in the present. You are no longer entangled in a repeating pattern but instead now have the space to breathe and choose the more effective and beneficial pathway for you and your circumstances.

SELF-COMPASSION

No one loves facing pain, let's be honest. Given that your brain's default is to shield you from it, it's not surprising that people carrying trapped pain wage a battle between wanting the hurt to end and wanting to avoid it. Wherever you are right now, regardless of what you have tried or denied, treat yourself gently and with kindness.

THE INTENTION

I encourage you to set an intention for yourself as you move through the Reset Program.

Your intention will remind you how it is that you want to show up for yourself and gently guide you when you veer a little off track or when you feel tempted to fall back into well-worn old habits.

Your intention can be as simple as: "I intend to be kind and compassionate with myself as I move through this program." Or it could be more specific, such as: "I intend to show up for myself in this way so that I can create the life I desire."

I encourage you to think deeply about what it is that you truly want, as your intention is a powerful tool. I invite you to write your intention down now and post it somewhere that you will see every day. This can be on your mirror in the bathroom, on the fridge, above your desk at work or even carry it around with you in your wallet or purse. Your intention should be something that is meaningful for YOU. It doesn't have to be anything grandiose, just something that will help you stay focused on what matters most to you, even when it gets hard.

My intention is to guide and support you through your journey to the very best of my ability.

Now that we've reached this foundational and fundamental first step of creating and holding intention together, I have complete confidence in your innate abilities to embrace the next step in your journey: Phase One of the Reset Program.

6.
PHASE ONE: SECURING YOUR BASE

HEALING IS A MATTER OF TIME, BUT IT IS
SOMETIMES ALSO A MATTER OF
OPPORTUNITY.

Hippocrates

You've made it! This is the foundational and most fundamental
first step in your journey, but you're not doing this alone. We will
be moving through every step of the way together, and I am
more than confident in you and your innate abilities to take on
this amazing next step.

It is in this phase of the program that you will learn to feel
comfortable within your own body, make a home for yourself
there and become friends with its physiological sensations.

I know there is an inherent desire to try to rush through
this phase to get to the processing and release phase. I know,
because I feel that pull too—the pull to just "get it over and

done with." It is normal to want to skip forward to the "feeling better" part, but it's critical that you don't rush this first phase.

Phase One is much like building your dream house. You're so excited—it's going to be the home you've always wanted! But then, to your dismay, you find out that the company that is going to put down your concrete foundation isn't able to schedule time with you for another three months. Instead of waiting, you decide to start putting up the walls and roof—a big job! Whenever you're looking at your brand new house from outside, you can't believe how amazing it looks. However, when you step through the doors, you immediately feel on edge. You can hear the house creak and groan with every whisper of wind.

A storm comes through one day, and suddenly the frame of the house lurches to one side, tipping over completely—roof and all. Your home has come crashing down around you. Without the solid foundation, it was simply the illusion of your dream home. You did not feel safe, comfortable or protected when you were inside. But to all those who walked past, including you, it looked like a picture of stability.

Patience is key when creating a solid foundation. It is not something that you can opt out of if you desire long-term, sustainable and meaningful change in your life.

Of course, if you decide to move quickly or skip forward through the work, you will still find some benefit. But, much like your dream house, without the solid foundation, there will be nothing supporting you should you encounter something triggering or stressful along your journey.

I know, I know—it sounds boring before you've even started, but trust me when I say, you will never regret taking the time necessary to create a solid foundation.

This phase is about removing the mystery, shame and stigma from your experience. Building knowledge helps you understand that your nervous system and brain are responding exactly the way they were designed to respond in order to survive.

Together we will begin to reclaim space by stabilizing your moods and building up a strong resource kit with which you can navigate challenging or distressing emotions, feelings or experiences. This will expand the range of situations and environments in which you are comfortable. These self-soothing techniques will allow you to reclaim your confidence in your ability to navigate daily life, feeling grounded and safe within the world.

PHASE ONE GROWTH

- Understanding safety

- Securing your base by becoming an objective observer

- Securing your base through reconnecting with your emotions

- Securing your base by nourishing your basic needs

- Securing your base with containment exercises

- Securing your base through your body

- Securing your base with regulating resources

Starting is the most overwhelming step in the journey, but this is your opportunity to provide yourself with the safety and stability that you may have never received, or that you need in order to give yourself solid ground to stand upon.

In return, give yourself the gift of slow, intentional movement and progress through Phase One. *Don't rush.* This is your opportunity. Take it!

UNDERSTANDING SAFETY

At their cores, healing and recovery are about regaining a sense of safety and control from within that spills over to the external environment around you. In your healing journey, establishing safety within yourself and your environment is the first task—the primary foundation for learning to heal from stress, anxiety and trauma.

The way you feel safe as an adult is heavily influenced by how your parents, family members and others treated, cared for and showed love when you were a baby and up until you were seven years old. A combination of past experiences, relationships and childhood exposure to various environments can contribute to your sense of safety. It may seem like a contradiction, but you can be in an environment that is objectively safe and still feel unsafe there. This happens because the way you learned to define safety no longer applies in your current situation.

If it's hard for you to feel safe inside, you may have found—or currently find—it useful to use your imagination to start helping your body feel safe (or at least safer), which is often the origins of dissociation, derealization and depersonalization.

It is important to distinguish between *being* safe—where you are not in physical danger—and *feeling* safe, which is a psychological expression of your nervous system.

You can feel physically safe, but not actually be in a situation where you're experiencing complete and total security. So focusing on how you feel—and shifting your ideas about what it means to feel "safe"—is the place to start when trying to change those sensations into something more congruent with your future goals or desires.

Safety definition

There are two dimensions to safety:

1. **Perception:** your experience of feeling safe and believing yourself to be safe.

2. **Reality:** objective markers that you are truly safe.

It can take time to learn how to *feel* safe! If you've spent a great deal of your life feeling unsafe, then it will probably take extra effort on your part—and possibly the help of others—to see that safety is something you're capable of creating.

SECURING YOUR BASE BY BECOMING AN OBJECTIVE OBSERVER

I want to share a core memory of mine that powerfully shaped my healing journey. In 2017, my now husband, Damian and I had been dating for about six months. At the time, I was living in a shared house with four other women, getting up at 4am every day to work in hospitality, then heading to uni to study psychology. In the evenings I had started to work on my business too.

Stressed and anxious was my default. I lived in a world where everything had to get done ASAP or it could all fall apart (or so I thought). The environment I lived in was also chaotic, with roommates coming and going, leases falling through and late payments the norm.

One evening, Damian came over to the house for dinner, and I asked him a simple question that would change the course of my life:

"Do you think I'm a negative person?"

Definitely a bold question to ask someone when your nervous system is going haywire and you really don't want to hear the answer.

He answered with honesty—that he didn't believe me to be a negative person, but the way in which I saw the world could oftentimes be skewed in a negative light.

You're right, I didn't *want* to hear the answer, but I *needed* to hear that from someone who I both looked up to and trusted. I definitely did not communicate how painful it was to hear these words at the time, and I subsequently didn't communicate how, from that point on, I began working extremely hard to shift this personal pattern.

The point is that I couldn't see this pattern until it was illuminated to me and, once I had the knowledge, or the mirror held up to me, I was able to begin to proactively work on it.

You see, when you're stuck in your own world, you never get

to take a breather. You never get to take a step back and see the whole picture. You're completely zoomed in, engulfed by the experience, people, thoughts, feelings and emotions. It's exhausting. But as soon as you can give yourself space, zoom out and truly objectively look at yourself from a shifted perspective, you can see the vast array of experiences of life that take place in every moment of every day.

One of the easiest ways that you can begin to reclaim this space is through a simple practice of record-keeping. This practice gives you the keys to zoom out, to look at yourself and your daily experiences from a different angle and to notice how you operate, who you are and the things you focus on.

For that reason, we are going to be learning together how you can become an objective observer of yourself—a formidable step in your healing journey.

Record-keeping

The first step of this program is to learn how you experience stress, anxiety and trauma—your symptoms, patterns and manifestations. You will keep a record as we go along so that you can spot any trends or connections in your own responses.

Throughout this program, no matter which phase you are in, consciously creating and maintaining records of your mood state among other things is very much encouraged for the purpose of self-awareness and reflection. This is your opportunity to learn about yourself in a safe environment where you are not judged, but supported.

The program is designed to support you in better understanding the nature and origins of your symptoms so that you can take ownership over them and begin making healthy changes in your life.

Keeping a record of your physiological, emotional and mental experiences on a regular basis can help you understand what triggers symptoms, as well as provide guidance for how to respond during future episodes.

When you experience intense or chronic anxiety, it can seem as if the feelings are out of control and have a life of their own. To gain control over those moments, you need to first create space and become an observer of your experience. This allows you to instil compassion where judgment or self-criticism once lived.

By keeping records of your symptoms and experiences, you will begin to notice patterns in the way they manifest.

This practice will build your self-awareness of the contributing factors that push you into states of arousal or shutdown. It can give you the map to allow you to tailor your strategies and resources to what you need in each moment.

In addition, you will learn to recognize various aspects of your daily experience within your nervous system: what it feels like when you are activated or low in energy; the thoughts that go through your mind at these times; the actions that result from those emotions.

The resources you find in this book are specially designed to help you access and regulate different nervous system states, including your emotions, thoughts and behaviors. You cannot support your nervous system, reset your vagus nerve or heal without a thorough understanding of the true nature of these experiences and states of arousal. Continually monitoring your moods and behaviors is more accurate than simply asking your-self how you're feeling.

If you were asked to describe the week that's just passed, you may judge it as a bad one based on how anxious and emotional you felt throughout that time. When we allow ourselves to dwell on our negative emotions without acknowledging any positive ones (or neutral ones), we can begin believing in an overly dramatic version of reality—one that doesn't accurately reflect what's really going on. Casting a negative light on the previous week, while overlooking what you've done well during that same time period, can contribute to feelings of anxiety and stress.

Recording your thoughts and moods on a regular basis helps you to see the ups and downs of your anxiety levels, as well as noting times when you feel less anxious than normal.

You may be worried that tracking your arousal levels will make you feel more anxious, stressed or overwhelmed, and this fear is understandable, particularly if you experience anxiety or worry about feeling anxiety or worry (in other words, if the anxiety feels as if it is out of your control). But I promise you that when you learn how to notice your arousal levels, you will feel empowered by being able to take charge of them. You will be able to use this information about what triggers anxiety for you as a way of making important decisions about your life and how to live it more intentionally.

How to monitor

We can monitor our moods in two ways: subjectively, by asking ourselves how we feel; and objectively, by using scales to rate the intensity of various emotions.

Subjective monitoring involves giving your personal assessment of the severity of your anxiety and if/how much you feel that there's no way to escape it. For many people, it's like trying to swim through a giant bowl of jelly—but you can't get out! Subjective monitoring is likely to be something you already do, and may be a habit that makes your anxiety worse.

Objective monitoring, which you will learn about in this lesson, is a more "scientific" way to effectively monitor the features of anxiety.

Rather than asking yourself, "How do I feel?" you will instead learn to record your experiences on a scale with a correlating number for the intensity of symptoms, for example, or honing in on your triggers as well as reflecting on the subsequent behavioral reactions that you had in response to different states of arousal.

Objective monitoring is like standing outside the giant bowl of jelly and noting its color, consistency and movements.

As you begin to monitor your feelings objectively, it may feel difficult or unnatural. However, with practice, the new way of monitoring will become automatic and second nature. In the beginning, you may still feel an increase in anxiety, stress or worry, but with consistent practice, you will slowly begin to shift from subjective to objective records.

You're probably thinking, *That sounds great, but I have no idea where to start!* Don't worry, I have you covered. To guide your record-keeping practice, I have created two very specific forms for you to photocopy/print out and make your own. We will go into a bit more detail about these two forms shortly.

First, let's review the benefits you'll enjoy as a result of your ongoing record-keeping:

1. Record-keeping allows you to identify specific factors that trigger your episodes of high anxiety, stress or survival responses; knowing these triggers and situations will lessen the feeling that you are at their mercy.

2. Record-keeping allows you to understand your own experiences of anxiety, stress and trauma more clearly and identifies *how* you experience those feelings in your body and mind.

3. Record-keeping gives you the ability to evaluate the resources and practices you put in place and how well they may be working for you. It also allows you to celebrate the wins and small gains you're making as opposed to getting stuck in negative thought patterns or rumination. When you have a bad day and then feel discouraged, look back at the records to see how far you've come.

4. Record-keeping allows you to become an objective observer of yourself, so that you can see your behavior from a distance. This is crucial for making real changes in your life.

Let's now have a look at the two records that you are going to be completing as you move through the rest of the program:

Worry Record

Your Worry Record is what you are going to use whenever you feel a shift in your arousal level. This could be anything from becoming aware that you're ruminating or overthinking. Maybe you can't sleep, you feel more tired than usual or you're experiencing muscle tension or brain fog. These are just a few examples, but there are many changes and shifts that you may experience that would be worthy of noting in your Worry Record.

The information you note down will be particularly helpful in beginning to uncover and understand your triggers, as well as how they feel both in the body and mind. It will also allow you to see how your behavior may be influenced or impacted by these experiences too.

At the top of the record, you're going to jot down the date and time (approximately) that you noticed your arousal level begin to change.

Then, objectively record the experience on the form by circling the maximum level of arousal that you felt.

On the same form, you'll also make a note about any symptoms you experienced that you can pinpoint. Although you may feel as though you experience these symptoms most of the time, it's important to distinguish if and when these symptoms may be felt more intensely or at certain times.

In the next portion of the record, you will then give a brief description of the triggers that may have contributed to this shift in arousal. These triggers could be such things as the time of day (like shortly before the end of a workday, when you start to worry about not having enough time to get everything done), reading an article in a newspaper about diseases that might affect your family members and yourself or not hearing back from someone in an expected time frame. If you're unsure about what triggered you, just write, "Don't know."

Then, in the "Anxious Thoughts" section, list what worries you most. Be as specific as possible in writing down your thoughts here—this part is very important!

Next, record how you cope with your worry—your behaviors. For example: pacing around the room, calling family members to check on them (even if they are feeling fine) or distracting yourself from worrying thoughts by engaging in a different activity.

Lastly, record when you first noticed your worry or physical sensations beginning to subside (at the top right corner of the Worry Record).

Daily Mood Record

Your Daily Mood Record is something that you are going to fill in at the end of each day, just before you head off to sleep.

This reflective practice uses a scale that rates levels of anxiety and physiological arousal on a scale from 0 (no anxiety) to 100 (extreme anxiety).

Write the date in the first column.

For the second column, simply record your average level of anxiety for the entire day by considering all of its events.

In the third column, record your highest anxiety level of the day. If that day you didn't experience any heightened states of activation or feel any low states of freeze or shutdown, then the numbers in this level will be the same as the second column.

In the fourth column, you're going to note down your

WORRY RECORD

DATE: _____ **TIME BEGAN:** _____ **TIME ENDED:** _____

Maximum level of anxiety (circle a number below):

0   10   20   30   40   50   60   70   80   90   100
NONE   MILD   MODERATE   EXTREME

Indicate which symptoms you are experiencing:

Restlessness, feeling revved up or on edge   ☐

Easily fatigued   ☐

Difficulty concentrating or mind going blank   ☐

Irritability   ☐

Muscle tension   ☐

Sleep disturbance   ☐

NAME and DESCRIBE YOUR PHYSICAL EXPERIENCE:

_____

_____

_____

TRIGGERING EVENT: **ANXIOUS THOUGHTS:**

_____   _____

_____   _____

_____   **BEHAVIORS:**

_____   _____

_____   _____

DAILY MOOD RECORD

Rate each column at the end of the day, using a number from 0–100 below

0   10   20   30   40   50   60   70   80   90   100

NONE   MILD   MODERATE   EXTREME

DATE	OVERALL ANXIETY	MAXIMUM ANXIETY	OVERALL PHYSICAL TENSION	OVERALL PREOCCUPATION WITH ANXIETY	

overall level of physical tension or discomfort. So, if you experienced any pain or aches in your body, had trouble focusing or felt restless or tired during the day, then take this into consideration as you record your score.

The fifth column is for recording where your mind went during the day, if you were stuck in overthinking, spiraling or intrusive thoughts. Reflect on your day and record how much of your time and energy was focused on these thought processes.

The sixth column is intentionally left blank in case you would like to monitor specific behaviors or patterns that are unique to you. For example, you may bite your nails or pick your skin and you can record these patterns using the same scale in this column.

In the beginning, reflecting and recording your daily experiences using these scales might feel a little odd, but over time they will become second nature to you. When you lean into using these scales, you can gain a far more objective overview of your physical experience and mood state as opposed to recording words or phrases about how you feel.

This is your first ritual of the program that you are forging, so it's important to set yourself small, achievable goals to maintain a level of consistency.

Try starting with a seven-day challenge of completing your Daily Mood Record each night before you go to bed. You could photocopy/print out the records and put them next to your bed with a pen to remind you to complete them!

If you miss a day, don't worry. You're human, and creating a new habit takes time. Remind yourself that you can just start again tomorrow: it's as simple as that!

SECURING YOUR BASE THROUGH RECONNECTING WITH YOUR EMOTIONS

Thoughts and emotions are not a choice. Just like breathing, they happen automatically. And, just like breathing, they are extremely vital and important to you as a human being and your ability to navigate the world.

I know that there are times when we would probably rather get rid of emotions entirely—the heaviness and pain that can be felt is sometimes immeasurable and overwhelming. But your emotions aren't just there to toy with you; your emotions are wise and beautiful teachers when you can begin to understand and listen to them. You don't have to be able to understand or explain what they mean right now—but if you can just quiet down and listen, they'll let you in on all the secrets that your body and mind are whispering beneath the surface.

Your emotions are the driver behind your behavior, which in turn determines your life experiences, the opportunities and risks that you take and the people who you create relationships with. Reconnecting with your emotions hands you the keys to understanding the language and internal dialogue of your nervous system, body and mind.

It's a worthy endeavor to take the time to notice what makes you feel good about yourself and the world around you, but also learn to acknowledge the sometimes unbearable pain that you may have felt through difficult experiences.

When you reconnect with your emotions, you can begin to speak the same language. You can begin to nurture yourself in truly nourishing ways. You can begin to rekindle intuition and body wisdom so that you always have a guiding light, a true north that will allow you to navigate life in a fulfilling and meaningful way.

You will also build self-awareness of the things in your life, your patterns, reactions and behaviors that may not be working so well for you, and then be able to gently guide yourself to a path that sits in alignment with your true desires and needs.

If you are struggling to notice or recognize your emotions, that's okay! Sometimes emotions are so subtle that it takes time to form vocabulary to describe them.

To physically feel an emotion, you need to slow down. This isn't a race, and struggling to tune into your emotion is not an indicator that there is anything wrong or broken.

People who experienced trauma early in life often experience feelings of numbness or lack of feeling. If this is your situation, please be reassured that it is a protective mechanism. It means that your body and brain are working perfectly to support your survival. You can learn to feel again. It's a gradual process, and it takes time to develop the ability to tune into your emotions.

If you have trouble identifying the emotions that you are feeling, start by identifying your physical sensations. Are there any sensations in your body that you can identify as physical feelings? Is your heart racing? Do you feel sick to your stomach? Is there tightness in the back of your neck or shoulders? What about a headache or sore muscles? These are all physical signs that something is going on for you emotionally, and identifying them is a great place to start as it begins to rebuild the connection between the body and the mind.

Emotions are not always easy to identify or describe. They

can be subtle, and it's okay if you don't feel like there's a word that exactly fits what you are experiencing. It's also okay if your emotion feels like a mix of different feelings: for example, feeling anxious but also angry or sad at the same time.

The most important thing is to simply begin to tune in—it's not about getting it "right," but about giving yourself the opportunity to connect with your own inner experience.

A note on trauma

Life experiences that happen in quick succession, chronic or ongoing stressors, going through challenging situations when support systems are absent and you are unprepared for change—these are all experiences of trauma to the nervous system, mind and body.

Trauma and life experiences can have a profound effect on the way we relate to ourselves and others, which intensifies emotional distress. But trauma does not take away your capacity to learn how to connect with your emotions once again. You are intrinsically built to heal. In other words, regardless of whether you feel completely disconnected from your emotions, with time, you can still reclaim this connection and skill. With gentle practice, you will slowly begin to be able to understand and express your emotions without becoming entangled within them. This is the key to reclaiming a sense of control and ownership in your own life and experiences.

As you develop and extend your capacity to identify and hold space for your emotions, you will notice a fundamental shift occur—greater self-compassion and awareness towards your emotions and how they might impact your body, mind and behaviors. You will find yourself connecting with others on a deeper level and improving your communication skills. This then allows you to build strong, respectful and mutual relationships with yourself and others in your life.

As you move through the Reset Program, that beautiful recognition of emotions and body signals will give you a strong foundation to guide the emotional regulation techniques to you and your unique needs.

You will also discover that your capacity for experiencing positive emotions grows and intensifies, bringing play, laughter and more moments of joy into your day-to-day life.

SECURING YOUR BASE THROUGH NOURISHING YOUR BASIC NEEDS

Put your hand up if you've ever said to yourself, "I'll start exercising tomorrow"—but when tomorrow rolled around, you didn't exercise at all …

There's no need to be ashamed. I have personally said this lots of times in my own life, only to have completely ignored the intention on the day in question! In a world where we are all busy, all the time, it's easy to see how taking action on the things that we fundamentally know will be beneficial for us can become exceptionally difficult and eventually be pushed to the wayside.

Between work, the never-ending bills, and trying to maintain relationships and some sort of semblance of health, we are always in pursuit of fulfilling our needs.

The needs that we are trying to fulfill were first put into

an easy-to-understand framework by Abraham Maslow. He suggested that the hierarchy of needs is as follows:

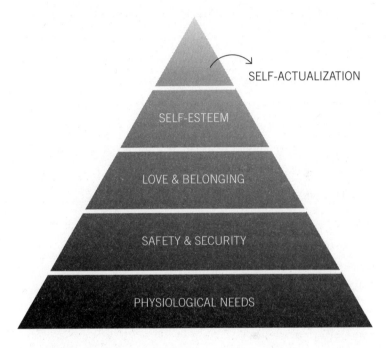

Each level builds on the previous one until you reach self-actualization at the top.

We will dive into these needs in greater detail in just a moment. The reason I am sharing Maslow's hierarchy of needs with you is because it's a simple way to begin to identify where in your life you may need to start to pay more attention and begin to nurture certain needs.

For most people—and you may recognize yourself in this—there is an innate desire to self-actualize—to be all that we can be, to pursue our passions and creative outlets. But what tends to happen is that, in this admirable pursuit, we forgo establishing the foundations that actually allow this to occur.

The same is true in the healing process. We want to process, release and just be "better," but without the foundations of your needs being met, you'll find yourself tumbling down more often than not.

This inevitably leads to feelings of defeat and helplessness, which is not what we are creating right here and now. No, what you are doing as you work through this phase of the Reset Program is building strong foundations that will create stability in all areas of your being and allow you to catapult your life in incredible and exciting ways that you can't even imagine at this point.

But in order to do that, you must first nurture your basic needs so that you are in a position to truly hold space for healing and reclamation to occur.

Let's take a deeper dive together into each of these human needs:

Physiological needs

These refer to physical needs like drinking water when thirsty and eating food when hungry. This also involves the physiological effort to maintain homeostasis in the body—that is, consistent levels of different bodily systems, such as maintaining a body temperature of 98.6°F.

Physiological needs are essential to your well-being because they involve basic physical functions like eating and sleeping. When you're extremely hungry, it's hard to think of anything other than food. And if you don't get enough sleep, you're more likely to be in a bad mood the next day.

Physiological needs also encapsulate your requirement for clean, breathable air, being able to adequately clothe yourself for the conditions, having secure and safe shelter over your head as well as reproductive choices.

Safety and security

Once your physiological needs are met, it is time to think about finding a safe environment.

In early childhood, children have a need for safe and predictable environments. When this want is not met, they are likely to react with fear or anxiety.

As adults, our need for a safe and predictable environment is as strong as ever. We still desire protection from violence and theft; we still want emotional stability and well-being, health support (including access to medical care) and financial security. All of these provide us with a feeling of control over aspects important to our lives.

Love and belonging

The next step is to meet your need for a sense of belonging and social connection. Humans are social creatures, and we need to feel part of something bigger than ourselves—to be loved as well as love others.

As children, we learn how to fit in with our peer group and develop relationships with friends and family members that provide us with a sense of belonging.

As adults, it is important for us to find places where we can make new friends or continue relationships with those from our past.

Researchers continue to explore how love and belonging needs impact well-being. Isolation, for example—feeling that you don't have social connections—is related negatively with physical health. Conversely, having strong relationships is associated with better physical health.

Self-esteem

Our need to feel good about ourselves—our self-esteem or pride in who we are as people—is an important part of our emotional lives and inner voice.

Self-esteem includes two components. The first kind of self-esteem is based on feelings of confidence and personal value. The second involves the recognition by others that your achievements have been important.

When your esteem needs are met, you feel confident and see yourself as worthy. But when they are not met, you become vulnerable to feelings of inferiority.

Self-actualization

Self-actualization is the desire to become all that you are capable of becoming. It is a quest for psychological growth, development and maturation. It's the feeling of fulfillment in life of following your authentic path.

It is a process of becoming, rather than simply being. In order to achieve your full potential, you need to be in touch with your feelings and emotions and be able to express them appropriately. You also need to develop an awareness of your own strengths and weaknesses as well as those of others.

Self-actualization is unique to each individual. For one person, it may mean helping others; for another, it might mean the achievement of a goal in an artistic or creative field.

Self-actualization can be defined as feeling that we are doing what we believe our purpose is.

Needs in constant motion

In much the same way that the phases in this book are dynamic and fluid, so too are your needs. You are constantly moving up and down the pyramid as you navigate the ups and downs of life. You may go through periods when you feel completely secure and loved and are pursuing your dreams. Then, at other points, you feel as though you are struggling to fulfill certain needs.

It's not a "one and done" scenario. In the same way that having one meal does not meet your physiological needs for the rest of your life, it's a constant and ongoing process to address and fulfill your needs.

As you were reading through these different needs, various sensations might have come up for you. Maybe some of those needs were uncomfortable or difficult to read as you reflected on your own current circumstances. Just remember that, no matter where you are in life currently, this is not the end of your story.

Together we are going to compile your own personal hierarchy of needs. Then you can begin to address these foundational and important needs in order to take the next steps in your healing journey.

Each and every one of us can find the tools to help us climb to the top of the pyramid.

Understanding your unique hierarchy of needs

In a moment, I am going to ask you to grab a journal, a piece of paper or a laptop and answer a few questions. It's important to take your time moving through these questions as this practice will illuminate any needs that may require a little more attention.

Journal your responses in a place that you can come back to. Remember that your needs are always on a continuum, so if you ever feel as though you're struggling or stuck, you can come back to this. Revisit your needs again and again.

Are you ready?

Physiological needs

Food
Do I have enough food to nourish my body and mind?

_____

Are there any avenues that can support this need? (Do you have access to family and friends to lend a hand, foodbank, social services, etc.?) List them below:

_____

_____

_____

Can I nourish my body in any way differently to honor my unique needs?

_____

_____

_____

Water
Do I have access to clean drinking water?

_____

_____

_____

Are there any avenues that I can explore to support this need?
List them below:

_____

_____

_____

Am I drinking enough water each day to support my body and
mind?

(Approximately 8–10 cups per day.)

_____

_____

_____

Sleep
What is my sleep like (overall)?

_____

Are there any avenues I can explore to support this need? List
them below:

_(Note these aspects of sleep hygiene: going to bed and waking up at
the same time; having a night-time ritual; reducing light sources at
night; eating at least two hours before bed; having a dark room;
reducing sound disturbances (using ear plugs); making sure your
environment is cool (64–65°F) for optimal sleep.)_

_____

_____

_____

_____

_____

Can I maximize the amount of sleep I am getting to support my body and mind?

_____

_____

_____

Safety and security

What is my environment like?

_____

_____

_____

What avenues can I explore to support this need?

_____

_____

_____

Can I put in place anything that will allow me to feel safer in this environment?

_____

_____

_____

Love and belonging

Do I have supportive and mutual relationships in my life?

_____

_____

_____

_____

_____

Are there any avenues that I can explore to support this need?

_____

_____

_____

Can I maximize my relationships in any way to enhance my sense of belonging?

_____

_____

_____

Self-esteem
How do I feel about myself?

_____

_____

_____

Do I feel valued by others?

_____

_____

_____

Are there any avenues I can explore to support this need?

_____

_____

_____

Can I take any intentional actions to enhance my self-esteem?

_____

_____

_____

SECURING YOUR BASE WITH CONTAINMENT EXERCISES

When I was little, any time I felt scared and heard loud noises or arguments, intuitively I tightly clasped my hands over my ears and around my head. Not only did this innate reaction dull the scary noises, but it also felt extremely soothing to enclose myself in this safe container. So much so, I found myself holding this position for much longer, even after the noise or fear had passed.

I didn't know at the time why it felt good, I just knew that it did.

As I grew into a boisterous teenager experiencing heartbreak and challenges, whenever I found myself curled up in an emotional ball, I would hold my head too.

You have probably observed examples of this behavior happening in a variety of circumstances. For example, when someone is shocked or surprised, they might fling their hands up to hold their cheeks. Or if someone is grieving or ill, they may hold their head or arms in a self-hug.

I wonder, do you notice any moments where you "hold" yourself? I know that for me, whenever I am feeling stressed or anxious, I seem to naturally place my left hand on my right shoulder unconsciously.

There is something about this action that, up until a few years ago, I never really questioned or explored all that much. But then I learned about containment, or self-holding exercises.

What is containment?

While experiencing heightened emotions, traumatic memories, anxiety or stress, we may feel scattered and broken. Our thoughts can become so overwhelming that they appear like chaos coming from every direction at once—completely out of our control.

These thoughts, sensations and emotions can feel exceedingly big, and begin to spill outside of ourselves, and that is where containment comes in.

Containment exercises are a simple-to-use self-holding technique that allows us to reclaim a sense of containment within our bodies and minds. They give you the power to take something that feels out of control, and physically reclaim a sense of control over yourself and the experience that is happening internally.

In a sense, you are reminding yourself that your body has edges—that the sensations, feelings and emotions that you are experiencing are all occurring within these parameters. In holding yourself, you feel a sense of these physical boundaries; you can feel your body; you can feel the energy occurring within its walls. And this has a calming effect on the nervous system because you begin to know through these sensations and the awareness of your physical edges that you are here, that you are in your body.

Interestingly, studies have found that certain types of touch, such as deep touch through cradling the head, can increase HRV (see page 24) and bring the ventral vagal system (see page 18) online.

So how can we use this knowledge to create safety when we are experiencing heightened emotions?

I am going to share with you five different self-holding and containment exercises that you can explore to see which one feels most soothing to you. I also encourage you to continue your exploration with these exercises by varying and changing the positioning to find the sweet spot that is unique to you. For some people, holding the back of the head may feel particularly soothing, but for others, it could be holding the forehead.

There is no wrong or right way of doing these exercises—only the way that feels best for you. So listen to your body as you are moving through these exercises to truly hear how you are responding.

Containment and self-holding exercises

Both hands can be placed in any of the positions below—do what feels most natural to you.

As you are going through these exercises, your task is to sink into the sensations that are moving through your body—just noticing, sensing and feeling; not exerting any energy to change or shift them. You may get a sense of the shape, color or energy of these sensations, or you may simply notice and name feelings as they come and go.

You can practice all of these positions in a sequence (one after the other) or you can choose one of these positions and practice it in isolation. Hold each position for at least 60 seconds or until you notice or sense a sort of shift happening within your body or mind.

Sides of head

Place your hands, palms down, on either side of your head. Think about how you are creating edges for the container that holds your thoughts—a sort of mental cubbyhole. Feel the sensation between these walls and notice them as they pass between your two hands.

Forehead and back of head

Place one hand on your forehead and the other at the base of your skull. Feel what's in between—where you hold all those thoughts that run through your mind.

Forehead and heart

Place one hand on your forehead and the other over your heart. Focus closely; be aware of any sensations between these two points.

Heart and stomach

Place one hand on your heart and the other on your stomach—either over, above or below your belly button; move your hand to an area that feels most comforting to you. Notice any and all sensations that move between these two areas of your body.

Middle of chest and base of skull

Find the point where your rib cage branches out in both directions (left and right) of your body. This space is above your belly button and just below the center of your rib cage. Place your other hand in the dimple at the base of your skull, slightly on your neck. Feel the sensation between these walls and notice them as they pass between your two hands.

SECURING YOUR BASE THROUGH YOUR BODY

When I was around 15 years old, my whole family went out for dinner at a restaurant. I ordered Singapore noodles, one of my favorite dishes!

While it tasted exceptionally delicious going down, what came afterwards was nothing short of harrowing. If you've ever experienced food poisoning, you know the feeling all too well; the sudden and severe realization that something is terribly wrong, followed by hours of bringing up every last ounce of content that your body may be holding.

Even after a substantial period of time had passed from that event, the next time I even saw the words "Singapore noodles" on a menu, it nearly made me every bit as sick. Why? I hadn't even touched the food, but every fiber of my being was saying, *Do not even think about this as a meal!* My body was making me physically sick at just the thought of the dish.

All of us have an inbuilt survival mechanism that is designed to remember anything that could potentially harm or cause a threat to our health and ultimate survival. Once something has been identified as threatening, the body will do anything in its power to make sure that the same situation does not happen again. The amygdala uses techniques like overgeneralization to make sure that our bodies and brains will respond as strongly to remotely similar threats.

In the case of food poisoning, the feeling of disgust is one of the strongest and immediate responses that the body and brain will conjure up in order to deter you from making the same mistake again.

This is true of all types of triggers, including people in our lives and environments who we encounter. In the case of a trusted person who hurt you (e.g., an abusive parent), this generalization may lead to the belief that other people are dangerous as well.

These triggers occur in a much more subtle fashion than food poisoning, but with reflection, we can see these broad generalizations stemming from experiences in all aspects of our lives. Then through your life experiences, this narrative becomes reinforced when people or environments cause hurt or pain. Through the accumulation of these experiences, our ideas and feelings of safety can become fractured. What or who once felt safe no longer does, so we shrink our idea of safety until it gets so small that even our own sensations, thoughts and feelings can feel unsafe and triggering.

In order to regain our personal sense of safety, we must first feel secure and confident in our own bodies.

Body-based exercises for establishing safety in the body

Bee breathing

Bhramari pranayama, or bee breathing, is an effective breathwork exercise to calm your mind and body. This type of breathing is named after the black Indian bee called Bhramari. "Pranayama" comes from two Sanskrit words: "prana," meaning life energy, and "yama," meaning control. When practicing this form of pranayama, you will notice that your exhalation resembles the sound of a humming bee.

Humming requires control over your inhalation and exhalation and can be used as a calming technique. Slowing down your exhale activates the parasympathetic nervous system. Many other studies show that slow, deep diaphragmatic breathing also reduces heart rate and blood pressure, while increasing HRV (see page 24).

In this exercise, using your voice also activates your vagus nerve, which is connected to your voice box (larynx).

1. Find a comfortable seated position with a straight back. Allow a gentle smile to fall across your face. You can complete this exercise with your eyes closed or drop your gaze to a few feet in front of you and soften your eyes.

2. Place your index fingers on the cartilage between your cheek and your ears (tragus).

3. Inhale slowly for a count of four and, as you exhale, make a humming sound like a bee. As you are humming, gently press the cartilage on the outside of your ear.

4. For best results, create a higher-pitched humming sound that you can feel vibrating through your lips, face and throat.

5. When you naturally finish your exhale, decompress your cartilage, pause for 2–3 seconds and then inhale again.

6. Continue this pattern 5–10 times.

7. Once you have completed all rounds, allow your eyes to remain closed or hold your softened gaze for up to a minute. Observe any sensations that you are feeling in your body.

Arm swings

Rhythmic movement is a fundamental aspect of human life. We breathe rhythmically, our bodies move in a circadian rhythm, our walking is rhythmic and even our chewing when eating follows a certain rhythm.

From the time we are in the womb, we are exposed to certain rhythmic patterns, such as a mother's heartbeat, and, as an infant, soothing rhythmic movements, such as rocking, calm our nervous systems and let us know that we are safe.

Rhythmic movements continue to be effective calming resources for us, even as adults. These movements use the vestibular (balance), proprioceptive (body awareness) and tactile systems, which have a calming and organizing effect on the brain and body.

1. Stand up straight with your arms hanging by your sides, feet shoulder-width apart.

2. Press off from your left foot, shifting your weight onto your right side. As you move your weight, swing your left arm across your body, wrapping it briefly over your right arm.

3. Then in a rocking motion, shift your weight from your right foot, back to your left, at the same time swinging your right arm across your body to your left side.

4. Continue this rhythmic movement for 3–5 minutes.

SECURING YOUR BASE WITH REGULATING RESOURCES

As we learned in Chapter 3, a regulated nervous system is a resilient nervous system, but how can you build resilience into your nervous system?

The first step to being able to regulate your nervous system is through deepening your awareness and understanding of your natural movements in and out of different nervous system states.

You might know that you're in an activated state of fight-or-flight, but you may have missed some of the triggers and physiological cues that led to you being in this state in the first place.

Mapping your nervous system may sound fancy, but it's an incredibly simple tool, especially because I know that, as you've been working your way through this phase, you have already started keeping your Daily Mood Records as well as your Worry Records (see pages 113 and 115). If you haven't started yet, that's okay, take this as your sign to do so now!

Adding a map of your nervous system to your toolkit is going to give you a truly holistic picture of your nervous system states—the triggers that may push you into certain directions of arousal (up or down), as well as begin to build out and hunt for your cues of safety (glimmers). On top of that, you will learn your unique way of experiencing each state, which allows you to build your body awareness and, in turn, tend to your individual needs.

How to map your nervous system

In order to map your nervous system, we're going to go through each state and write down a few words that help you recognize and build awareness of that state.

But before we jump into the map, turn back to page 18 for a reminder of the three states of the nervous system according to polyvagal theory: fight-or-flight, dorsal vagal and ventral vagal. Below you'll also find a quick vocabulary crash course on two other important terms:

Triggers

A trigger can be anything from a person, place or thing—or even an event or situation—that evokes in you a strong emotional or physiological response. A sensory stimulus can be a trigger: anything from the smell of cookies baking to seeing someone with red hair (because it reminds you of an ex) may set off this sort of reaction.

Glimmers

The term "glimmer" was first coined by Deb Dana (licensed clinical social worker, consultant, author and speaker specializing in complex trauma). Glimmers are small moments that spark joy, serenity or peace. These can help cue our nervous system to stay calm and relaxed when we experience them. Your glimmers can be anything: a smile from a stranger, the full moon shining brightly in the sky or hearing your favorite song on repeat. These small moments bring you back to a space of safety within your nervous system.

Each of the three different states, along with the triggers and glimmers, are going to make up your nervous system map. So now all we have to do is actually map your nervous system. Are you ready?

Answer the following questions as best you can. If you feel stuck or overwhelmed at any point, just take a pause and come back to it when you feel as though you have a bit more space to do so.

My nervous system map

My triggers are:
List anything you can think of that pushes you out of feeling safe, calm or grounded.

1. **Example:** When someone doesn't let me know that they're going to be late.

2. _____

3. _____

4. _____

5. _____

6. _____

7. _____

8. _____

9. _____

10. _____

My glimmers are:

List anything that brings a natural smile to your face. What gives you the warm fuzzies? What makes you feel connected?

1. **Example:** When I see a stranger doing a good deed.

2. _____

3. _____

4. _____

5. _____

6. _____

7. _____

8. _____

9. _____

10. _____

When I am in fight-or-flight, I feel:

List any sensations, feelings, emotions, thought patterns or behaviors that you notice when you're in a state of hyperarousal.

1. **Example:** I feel a chaotic energy bubbling beneath the surface.

2. _____

3. _____

4. _____

5. _____

6. _____

7. _____

8. _____

9. _____

10. _____

When I am in dorsal vagal (shutdown), I feel:

List any sensations, feelings, emotions, thought patterns or behaviors that you notice when you're in a state of hypoarousal.

1. **Example:** I feel a sense of weight and heaviness in my body, like I can't move.

2. _____

3. _____

4. _____

5. _____

6. _____

7. _____

8. _____

9. _____

10. _____

When I am in ventral vagal (parasympathetic), I feel:
List any sensations, feelings, emotions, thought patterns or behaviors that you notice when you're in a ventral vagal state.

1. **Example:** I feel present—focused but not fixated.

2. _____

3. _____

4. _____

5. _____

6. _____

7. _____

8. _____

9. _____

10. _____

Amazing! You have just mapped your nervous system, which means that not only have you actively increased your self-awareness and body awareness, but you've taken the first step in regulating your nervous system!

The next piece of the puzzle is to build out a kit of regulating resources that you can use for different states that you find yourself in.

What I mean by that is, what works for a state of activation (fight-or-flight) won't necessarily be the right tool for when you find yourself in a dorsal vagal (shutdown) response.

Mapping your nervous system gives you back the ability to nurture each state based on your unique needs and desires. Below we'll go over three resources for hyperarousal states (fight-or-flight) and three resources for hypoarousal states (dorsal vagal).

But I want you to keep an open mind. Throughout this phase you have learned many different resources for creating safety: for example, containment exercises. You might find that containment exercises work really well for you when you're in an activated state. I want you to honor that intuitive nudge. If containment exercises feel best for you, then they can be your regulating resources for hyperarousal.

It's all about exploration. Think of yourself as a mad scientist: you're trying lots of different and new tools and experimenting as much as possible. If something doesn't work for you, that's okay! It doesn't mean anything about you personally; it simply means that it's not the right tool for you at this moment. If that's the case, you move on to try something else.

Sounds good?

Hyperarousal regulating resources

- **Proprioceptive sensory input:** Proprioceptive stimulation is the body's ability to locate the position in space as the body moves—think pressure receptors. It can be stimulated with weight-bearing (push-ups, crawling), resistance activities (pushing, pulling), heavy lifting, cardiovascular (running, jumping), oral (chewing) and deep pressure (hugs!). Bear in mind that whichever of these activities you do is beneficial not only for your body but also for your nervous system.

- **Cold exposure:** Cold exposure lowers stress hormones and downregulates amygdala activation. It has been proven to improve depression, anxiety and other mood disorders, and regulate the nervous system. It also speeds metabolism and improves immune responses in many cases. Try having a cold shower, a cold face plunge or placing a cold ice pack wrapped in a thin cloth on your chest and cheeks.

- **Singing:** The vagus nerve is connected to your vocal cords and the muscles that are at the back of your throat. This means that singing, chanting, humming or gargling all have the ability to put you into rest and digest mode. It can activate your vagus nerve and positively influence your mind—whether you prefer to sing in the shower or join the chorus!

Hypoarousal regulating resources

- **Natural light exposure:** The bright colors of the sun have the ability to calm your nerves. They also help to regulate the circadian rhythm through melatonin production and lower cortisol levels. While being in the sunshine, the number of neurotransmitters, such as serotonin, increases, which has positive results for our well-being. When the sun is out, spend 5–10 minutes outside at various times throughout the day. If it's overcast, plan on spending 20–30 minutes outside to increase your exposure.

- **Relaxing music:** Music can help activate the parasympathetic nervous system by helping relax the mind. Listening to slow music decreases blood pressure and heart rate, as well as respiration rate. There are specific musical frequencies that have more benefits for our minds and bodies than others. Some studies show that listening to music at a frequency of 432Hz—which is about 100 cycles per second lower than the 440Hz standard tuning most modern-day instruments use— produces calming responses in listeners when compared with higher-pitched tones such as those produced by 440Hz.

- **Take a hot shower or bath:** Studies have shown that soaking in a hot bath can calm the body by reducing sympathetic nervous system activity. Adding Epsom salts to the water increases magnesium levels, which also induces relaxation. To make the bathing experience even more enjoyable, you can add a few drops of essential oil to your bath water and play some relaxing music. This way, you will engage all of your senses in this soothing activity.

HOW TO INTEGRATE THE PRACTICES

In this phase, we have moved through many steps, tools and resources that can be used to come back to your body as a safe space and anchor. This forms the groundwork, the solid foundation, the secure base beneath your feet that will tether your mind and body to allow you to continue to explore your experiences, sensations, thoughts and emotions as you move into Phase Two of the program.

In exactly the same way that the concrete foundations of a new house need time to set and cure, so do these new practices and resources that you have learned. In order for these practices, tools and resources to create real and powerful change in your life, they must become integrated into your daily habits.

Integration is the most crucial step in your healing journey, but because we are often in a rush to move forwards, it's commonly overlooked. In order for integration to occur, we need two key ingredients: repetition and consistency.

It is not realistic for you to practice daily every single tool that has been shared in Phase One. That would almost certainly be completely overwhelming and time-consuming, and it is most definitely not encouraged. Instead, I urge you to create a realistic plan that integrates the practices that resonate most with you.

To help get you started on what this may look like, I have broken down the list of practices into three categories: daily practices, one-off practices and when-needed practices:

Daily practices
- Daily Mood Record (night)
- Containment exercise (choose one—practice daily)
- Body exercises (choose bee breathing or arm swings—practice daily)
- Regulating resources (choose one)
    - proprioceptive
    - cold exposure
    - singing
    - natural light
    - relaxing music
    - hot shower or bath

One-off practices (but revisited intermittently)
- Nourishing your basic needs journal exercise (create action items)
- Mapping your nervous system (write down list of glimmers and keep handy)

Practices for when needed/desired
- Worry Record
- Recognizing and sitting with emotions
- Hyperarousal regulating resources (choose one)
    - proprioceptive

- º   cold exposure
- º   singing
- Hypoarousal (choose one)
  - º   natural light
  - º   relaxing music
  - º   hot shower or bath

This is just an example of how these practices can become integrated into your day-to-day life without becoming overwhelming. You are encouraged to take this and make it your own, which means looking at your daily habits and routine and finding where these practices make the most sense for you.

It's also vitally important that you continue with these practices, even as you move into Phase Two. Phase Two will build on these practices, and they will continue to be a part of your plan and structured routine.

7.
PHASE TWO: RECLAIMING YOUR BODY

INTELLIGENCE IS PRESENT EVERYWHERE IN OUR BODIES ... OUR OWN INNER INTELLIGENCE IS FAR SUPERIOR TO ANY WE CAN TRY TO SUBSTITUTE FROM THE OUTSIDE.

Deepak Chopra

Phew! You did it—you are now in Phase Two! You've just undergone some major groundwork throughout Phase One of building and securing a really solid base for yourself to take big steps forward.

I am so incredibly proud of you and you should be too. Take a moment to really just celebrate yourself right here and now. It's not easy to do the work, but you're here, nurturing your nervous system and giving yourself lifelong tools and resources that are going to absolutely change the way in which you move through your day-to-day.

Before you take your next steps, I encourage you to reflect for a moment. How do you feel? How does it feel to be inside your body? Did you notice any shifts or changes occur as you were working through Phase One? I ask you these questions because Phase One of this program is not just a small piece of the puzzle, but rather an act of reclamation—you reclaim yourself. It takes courage and self-respect to move through at your own pace and time frame.

Believe me, I know how tempting it can be to rush through these phases and move from one to another, but each of these steps is circular. That means that you can go back and forth between them more than once—each time deepening your knowledge of the practices and cementing their foundation in your life.

If there's any hesitation, resistance or feeling of instability still lingering for you right now, that's okay. I want you to circle back to Phase One and allow yourself the time and space to really allow these deep practices of safety to sink into your skin and down to your very core.

If you're feeling confident and secure at this point, then you're ready to take the brave next step into Phase Two of building body awareness and welcoming in release of past experiences.

This phase is about deepening your connection to all parts of your body and mind, blowing off the dust from the dark corners that we've kept hidden away and clearing the cobwebs to welcome those parts back into the light of day.

You will be reclaiming your body as your home, as well as the sensations and feelings that come with it, and beginning to release the grip of the past that continues to play out in this present moment through movement, touch and sound.

You will gently weave all parts of yourself together as a whole, and welcome in your emotions as wise and beautiful guides of release and connection.

The techniques that you learn in this phase will be carried with you as you move and transition through life, offering respite and space from big, sticky and often heavy experiences and emotions. You will expand your nervous system's capacity and build resilience into your very core so that you feel as though you are able to ride the waves of life with ease.

PHASE TWO GROWTH

- Cultivating a strong mind-body connection through self-trust

- Understanding body awareness

- Reclaiming your body with conscious movement

- Reclaiming your body with restorative yoga

- Reclaiming your body with balance exercises

- Reclaiming your body through mindful attention

- Reclaiming your body through somatic release

CULTIVATING A STRONG MIND-BODY CONNECTION THROUGH SELF-TRUST

As we touched on in Chapter 4, self-trust is the foundation of all things. It's the bedrock that supports every other part of your life, and it's what allows you to build a strong connection to yourself—and then extend that connection outwards into the world around you.

Self-trust is an important skill to cultivate, and it can take time. It's also a journey that never ends: as we continue to explore ourselves and our experiences, we will find new ways to trust ourselves more deeply. The goal isn't perfection—it's progress.

When you trust yourself, you know that you have the strength and ability to get through anything life throws at you. Self-trust is what allows you to take chances, make decisions and follow your heart. It means that you are willing to be honest with yourself, even when it's difficult or painful. And that's where the work begins. Building self-trust isn't easy—it takes practice, effort and patience.

When you don't trust yourself, however, it can feel like everything is a struggle—and that's because it *is* a struggle! If you don't believe in yourself enough to think that things will work out in the end; if you don't feel secure enough to know that everything will be fine, no matter what happens; if you don't have faith in your own abilities and judgment … well then, how do you expect *anyone else* to have faith in you?

That's why self-trust is so important—it gives us the confidence we need to connect with others on an emotional level. When we know our own minds well enough and are comfortable with who we are inside, we feel safer in our own skins.

That sense of security lets us be more open with other people, which makes it easier for them to love us back.

Building self-trust requires self-awareness, reflection and self-compassion. It involves acknowledging and accepting your strengths and weaknesses, and learning from past experiences.

Taking risks and making mistakes are part of the learning process. By doing these things, we become more confident and resilient. You could even say working through this book and learning about your nervous system is a risk in a sense—as you're trying something completely new, which can be scary.

As we learn more about ourselves and our relationships with others, we build a stronger sense of self-trust. When we know what makes us happy, sad, angry or scared, it's easier for us to take care of ourselves and make good choices that benefit us in the long run.

Self-doubt, shame and perfectionism are three of the biggest barriers to self-trust. When we're caught up in these feelings, it's hard to believe in ourselves and our abilities.

We might think that other people are better than us or that we don't deserve what we want. We might feel like we're not good enough, or not smart enough, or not pretty enough—and those feelings can make us feel like we can't be led by or trust our own instincts.

Self-doubt can make it hard to take action or try something new. It makes you feel like a failure even before you've tried anything at all. It's the kind of doubt that tells you to cancel plans with friends because they'll probably see through your facade and realize what a fraud you are.

Just like self-doubt, shame can be debilitating. It's the feeling that we're not good enough for other people or will make them uncomfortable due to our perceived flaws. Shame makes us believe we're flawed, worthless and unlovable—and that no one would want to be around us if they really knew what was going on inside.

Perfectionism—a tendency to set impossible standards for ourselves and then punish ourselves when we fail to meet those expectations—is a form of self-sabotage. When you're stuck in a perfectionistic mindset, it can seem like there's no way out. It's easy to get caught up in comparing yourself with others and feeling like you're always falling short, eroding trust in yourself and your abilities.

Feeling self-doubt, shame and perfectionist tendencies are normal, natural human experiences from time to time, but when they become the go-to response when life becomes challenging, it is a key indicator that you don't wholly trust in yourself, your innate wisdom or your body.

Reclamation starts with feeling: *feeling* your body, *feeling* the emotions that weren't able to course through you before, *feeling* that sense of this is me, this is my body, this is my home. But reconnecting with that felt sense requires a certain level of trust.

The definition of trust is the firm belief in the reliability, truth or ability of someone or something.

If you haven't felt your body for a long time, then you may not trust the sensations and feelings that it produces.

If you haven't felt certain emotions or you've spent a good amount of energy on keeping certain emotions at bay, then you will not trust that you truly have the capacity to feel them completely.

We have to reclaim a sense of trust within ourselves, our abilities and capacity to handle all that we are, as well as begin to reclaim a sense of trust in others, in order to reclaim ourselves as we are designed and have the potential to be.

Trust can only occur when there is a level or sense of familiarity. When you are familiar with something or someone you often feel a sense of comfort or certainty. In essence, trust is found when we feel safe.

When we work with our bodies—paying attention to how they feel, what emotions are stirred up by different sensations or experiences and noticing the internal dialogues that often run silently in our heads—we can begin to break down barriers of shame.

When we begin to connect with our bodies, and become aware of the many ways in which they represent our inner lives, we can begin to heal old wounds, build new foundations and cultivate a deep sense of self-trust.

As you begin to trust yourself, this spills over to create trust within others, allowing you to nurture healthy and respectful social connections and relationships.

We have an evolved capacity for sociability that makes us want to form and strengthen relationships with other people and the world around us. This is a powerful force, and one that benefits both you and the people around you. When you trust yourself, you can better trust others, expanding your sense of safety to outside of yourself and beyond.

Self-trust is the beginning of your reclamation journey, and it's the first step to reclaiming your power and sense of self-worth. By learning how to trust yourself, you can begin to create a life that feels authentic and true to who you are at your core.

WHAT IS BODY AWARENESS?

Being aware of your body seems like a strange thing to focus on. I mean, I know I have a body—shouldn't that be enough?

The term "body awareness" was not something that I had even come across until a few years ago, when I was struggling with a particularly annoying symptom of anxiety. I kept losing feeling in my hands, like I had pins and needles. But this feeling would spread all up my arms, legs and through my face. It would be so uncomfortable—to the point that the sheets on my bed would feel physically painful touching my skin. I found myself being clumsy, too. I would accidentally cut my finger when slicing an apple and wouldn't even really notice until I saw the blood.

This feeling was driving me wild. I went and saw doctor after doctor and had a million and one blood tests, only to be told, "You're fine." It was infuriating, debilitating and overwhelming all at once. How could I feel like I was dying but have absolutely nothing "wrong" with me?

This feeling would come and go, until I noticed a pattern in it. When I was really anxious or stressed, the tingling would start to creep up through my fingers and into my body. Okay, so there was a connection to stress that I hadn't noticed before.

Then I started to play with it a little bit: I would sit there with my hands absolutely pulsing with pins and needles and press my fingers together, telling myself, "These are my fingers" over and over again. That seemed to help too.

Eventually, after many years of experiencing this uncomfortable sensation, I found breathwork. I felt like I had a sudden realization: that for most of my life, since I was ten years old and in the roller coaster accident, I had been breathing in a dysfunctional way. This pattern of overbreathing (hyperventilation) and holding my breath, along with breathing through my mouth, had created the perfect storm for my body to create an imbalance between the oxygen and carbon dioxide in my blood—particularly in my extremities—resulting in pins and needles sensations.

This breathwork journey spanned many years of my life, but what it taught me was the practice and importance of body awareness.

Body awareness helps you feel where your body is in space, how it moves and what conditions (such as pain) are affecting the way it functions. As a result, this ability can be essential when performing tasks like driving or playing sports.

Body awareness helps us understand how we should interact with objects and other people. For instance, when reaching for something on a high shelf, we intuitively know the distance at which to grab it.

Body awareness also gives you the capacity to notice the sensations, feelings and movements of your body, like your breathing patterns, and allows you to "course correct." For example, when I realized that I had a dysfunctional breathing pattern, I made it a goal to notice and change my breathing regularly throughout my day. Or when I noticed the pins and needles sensation (awareness), I then had the capacity to change my physiology through my breath.

Body awareness primarily uses two systems: the proprioceptive system, which includes the muscles and tendons, and allows you to know where your limbs are as they move; and the vestibular system in your inner ear, which helps you maintain balance.

The vestibular system is the part of your inner ear that controls balance, posture and head stability. If you feel dizzy or off-balance it's a good bet that the vestibular system is experiencing an issue.

Body awareness can include an understanding of your body's needs. For example, you realize that you're hungry or thirsty. It also covers noticing needs like social connection or spending time on your own or when you feel like you need to exercise or move your body.

Experiences like trauma, anxiety and stress can diminish our body awareness, because being in our body or being aware of the sensations and messages that our bodies are sending us can become frightening, triggering and overwhelming.

As humans, we tend to block out or build walls around parts of ourselves that feel painful to touch, and that includes our connection to our bodies. Over time, this disconnect means that we aren't able to care and nurture ourselves in meaningful, compassionate and healthy ways. We begin to create behaviors and patterns specifically to avoid certain feelings or sensations.

Part of your healing journey towards reclamation is reconnecting deeply with your body in its entirety—reconnecting with the sensations and feelings, the messages and the nudges that your body sends to you.

Through building body awareness, we regain the capacity to hold our bodies in a way that is confident. We understand ourselves more deeply and begin to trust our bodies to carry us; we build our intuition as we listen and decipher the messages our bodies send to us.

Why building body awareness is beneficial

Recognizing what we feel and why we feel that way gives us the ability to regulate our emotions and control our lives.

If we have conscious awareness of what's going on in our minds and bodies, we can choose to respond differently than we normally would. Instead of getting caught up in habitual reactions—like becoming overwhelmed by sensations or experiencing sweating or a racing heart when speaking to large groups—we might notice these feelings without letting them take over.

When we mindfully tune into the physical sensations that arise within us, we gain insight into what is going on inside and become capable of taking care of ourselves.

Our body has sensory neurons that respond to stimuli like changes in heart rate or breathing, damage to cells and tissues, movement around joints and muscle contraction. These sensory receptors send information about a change in our internal state to our brain for processing. For example, if I ask you to notice how your second and third toes feel, can you? Did moving them help with that at all?

Building your body awareness hands you back the keys of control. You can innately listen, understand and nurture your internal experience, which inherently allows you to feel more confident in your external world.

There are many benefits of increasing your own body awareness, including:

Strong mind–body connection

Body awareness strengthens your connection between your mind and body (see page 70). When you know and feel where your body is in space, you can better direct it to do what you want—and enjoy doing so!

Pain management

Research suggests that mindful awareness of your body may reduce pain.

Suppressing bodily sensations has been shown to lead to:

- low self-esteem
- physical isolation and less physical contact with others
- symptoms of depression

Individuals with pain or chronic pain who use mind–body techniques tend to have a higher level of compassion and connection with their bodies. In turn, this creates higher levels of self-acceptance, less sensory pain and increased feelings of energy and vitality.

Recognizing and nurturing your needs

Body awareness gives you the capacity to tune into the cues your body is sending you. This information gives you a greater understanding of what you need from moment to moment. You can recognize and respond to cues of thirst, hunger, emotional pain or distress in real time with conscious and mindful action.

When you understand what your body is communicating, it can help you better meet your own needs—and the result is greater health and emotional satisfaction.

Enhanced mental and emotional well-being

When the information that we are receiving from the environment through our proprioceptive and vestibular systems isn't correct— for example, when our body feels like it's moving when we're actually still, or vice versa—it can be extremely stressful, setting off alarm bells in the body and mind.

Being in tune with your inner and outer environment can help you feel more secure. This heightened body awareness has been shown to result in an array of health benefits, including:

- reducing symptoms of anxiety and depression
- reducing episodes of vertigo

Overall, building your body awareness gives you an anchor, a resource that you can lean on to learn about the state of your nervous system, mind and body. Creating body awareness builds your sense of self-trust and confidence in your body and mind to handle challenges, transitions and difficult or stressful moments in a calm and conscious way.

It gives you the starting point to be able to communicate your needs more effectively, allowing you to deepen your connections and relationships with those around you.

One last beautiful benefit, before we dive into some activities, is that building your body awareness reduces the fear that can come up with sensations.

For some, this may be a fear that takes hold when you feel your heart rate increase; for others, it may be that sick feeling in your stomach. Through building your body awareness, you disentangle old, unhelpful narratives that you have attached to these sensations and feelings, and begin to view and decipher these messages in a more constructive and helpful light.

So are you ready to reconnect with your body? Let's go!

RECLAIMING YOUR BODY WITH CONSCIOUS MOVEMENT

One of the most effective ways to create change within the body and build body awareness is through conscious movement. Physical change driven by gentle movement stimulates the sensory system; this is one reason why movement helps in trauma recovery.

Slow, conscious activity that gently shifts your physiology is best for building body awareness as it gives you the space and time to process sensations and emotions.

Intense or rapid physical action can be overwhelming and stressful, making it more difficult to become aware of your internal bodily sensations.

It's an art form to train yourself to pay attention to sensations like stretch, pressure, discomfort and movement—just staying completely present in the action you are performing or posture you are holding.

When was the last time you were completely focused on one thing?

When it comes to building body awareness, what I am really asking of you is to pay attention; to tune into your body not from the perspective of a particular goal, but from an active listening standpoint.

If someone you love is in front of you and they are sharing something they are excited about, but you have headphones in while listening to a podcast, you're not going to hear what they're saying.

Your body is no different. If you're performing an exercise but in your mind you are thinking about what you're having for dinner or whether you're doing the movement correctly, then you're not truly listening to your body.

Below you will find three somatic practices to explore. Some of these may resonate with you more than others, and that's okay.

You can choose one of these practices to begin with, or several; whichever ones sound most interesting and feel like a good fit for you.

If you enjoy one of these practices, continue doing it two or three times per week. If one practice doesn't resonate with you, then try another. Trust your inner guidance.

If you're feeling discomfort in a practice, ask yourself whether that's something you can work with or whether it is more beneficial to hit pause on this practice and come back to it at a later date when you're feeling more comfortable within your body and mind.

Let each new practice unfold at its own pace. There is no need to rush; your only goal is to be in touch with what's happening inside you as you do the practices.

Throughout the exercises that we are going to work through below, I want you to come back to a simple set of prompts:

- What (if any) sensations do you feel right now?
- Explore the language that you can give to these sensations.
- Do you feel tight, loose, chaotic or calm? Do you feel a sense of tingling, coolness or warmth? Do your muscles feel soft or hard?

Use language to give colorful or descriptive words to these sensations.

If you can't feel anything at all, that's okay too. You may feel numb, which is a sensation in itself and a beautiful starting point.

Gentle movement can be a lovely way to release emotions and let go of pent-up energy, and could include dancing in a way that feels good for you, shaking it out or finding movements that are so soothing they feel relaxing to perform.

As you move, bring your attention to the sensations in your body, noticing how they change as you breathe. Try to move slowly, allowing yourself time to feel each movement and sensation that comes up.

Swaying

1. Stand with your hands at your sides, legs comfortably apart, knees gently bent. Shift the weight of your body to one foot and feel it cross over the midline of your body.

2. Cue into the awareness of slow movement and then very slowly move back to the midline where you notice complete body balance. Once this has been achieved, continue moving slowly onto your other foot.

3. Allow your attention to consciously shift to your breathing, slowly inhaling through the nose and elongating your exhale to the rhythm of your movement.

Rocking

Rocking can help activate the vestibular system, which controls our balance and spatial orientation. The body adapts to the changing perspectives and begins developing a sense of balance.

The vestibular system, which is responsible for processing sensory information from the inner ear and transmitting that data to our brains, develops rapidly when we are young. This may be why rocking seems so fundamental during childhood—it's such an effective way of stimulating this critical part of our bodies!

Whether we were rocked to sleep as babies or spent summer days joyfully rocking back and forth on a rocking horse, our early experiences of gentle motion have shaped us all. After we've grown out of cribs and playgrounds, it's much harder to find opportunities to engage our vestibular system—though the need for such engagement does not disappear.

To gently engage your vestibular system, you can rock back and forth in your chair, use a rocking chair or gently sway while standing up.

Swinging

1. Stand with your feet shoulder-width apart on a stable surface.

2. Begin by rotating your torso to the left. Your arms should hang loosely at your sides and will move only because of the momentum of your body moving—not because you consciously decide that it needs to happen.

3. When you've turned as far to the left as you comfortably can, turn in the opposite direction, swinging your arms loosely along with your body.

4. As you continue to turn from side to side, your arms will begin slapping lightly against your body.

5. Continue this swinging movement for 3–5 minutes, tuning into the sensations throughout your body.

RECLAIMING YOUR BODY WITH RESTORATIVE YOGA

Restorative yoga is a therapeutic form of yoga that focuses on gentle, slow and conscious movements and focuses on the breath to create a space for healing. Restorative yoga is particularly beneficial for activating the parasympathetic nervous system and vagus nerve and restoring balance between the body and mind.

In restorative yoga, you hold positions or poses for longer, allowing your body to ease and sink into postures, often coupled with deep breathing practices that activate the relaxation response. Deep breathing stimulates the vagus nerve, which, as we explored in Chapter 1, runs from the brain to the abdomen and is responsible for inducing a relaxed state.

Ideally, you'll need a yoga mat to practice the following yoga poses. If you do not have a mat, you can practice on the floor using a towel laid out flat instead.

Child's pose

This pose helps release stress, fatigue and tension in your body. It gently stretches the muscles along your spine—as well as those in your hips, glutes (buttocks), hamstrings (back of thighs), legs and shoulders.

Using a pillow or blanket can also help to alleviate neck or back pain and support head and spine alignment.

1. Kneel on the mat with your knees hip-width apart and your buttocks resting on your heels. Bring your big toes together so they are just touching one another under your buttocks.

2. You can make yourself more comfortable by placing a cushion or folded blanket between your thighs and calves.

3. Exhale and lean forward until your torso is between your thighs, then lower your head down towards the mat.

4. Place your palms on the mat and extend your arms out in front of you, over your head. If this is uncomfortable for you, place your arms by your legs, with your palms facing up.

5. To make yourself more comfortable, you can add a pillow or folded blanket under your head and arms.

6. Inhale through your nose, allowing your belly to expand outwards and exhale slowly through your nose or mouth while in the pose for up to five minutes.

7. Gently release this pose by bringing your hands underneath your shoulders and lifting your torso back up into a seated position.

Savasana

In savasana (corpse pose), a completely relaxed state of mind is not necessarily the goal. Rather, it's important to relax with attention—remaining conscious and alert while relaxed, in order to become more aware of long-held tensions in our body and mind.

Savasana is a practice of gradually relaxing one body part at a time—one muscle, then another. It helps you release stress and improves your sense of physical and emotional well-being when done regularly.

1. Place a folded blanket at the top end of your mat, and another folded blanket or two stacked on top of each other near the bottom of your mat.

2. Find a position in between the folded blankets and come to a seated position with your knees bent and back straight.

3. Extend your legs, so that the backs of your knees are putting their full weight resting on the folded blanket(s) at the bottom end of your mat.

4. Gently roll your spine backwards onto the mat, resting your head on the blanket at the top of your mat.

5. Allow your arms to find a natural position by your sides, allowing for a gap between your arms and your body.

6. Starting at the top of your head, allow your crown, forehead and eyes to soften and relax.

7. Move through each part of your body, allowing it to soften and relax, all the way down to your toes.

8. Remain in this position for ten minutes or more. Focus on your breath, inhaling through the nose, expanding the belly outwards towards the ceiling, exhaling through the nose or mouth and allowing your belly to relax towards the floor.

RECLAIMING YOUR BODY WITH BALANCE EXERCISES

Improving your balance builds your coordination and strength, making it easier for you to move freely. It also enhances stability, mobility and flexibility—all of which will help you perform daily tasks more easily. It also increases your ability to focus by training you to clear your mind and tune into your body.

Balance exercises make you more aware of where your body is at all times. This allows your nervous system to control and coordinate all its muscles so that you can move in space accurately.

Greater coordination also builds your body awareness. Balance exercises train your nervous system to become more efficient at controlling joints and muscles—resulting in smoother, more coordinated and confident movements.

Below are several exercises and drills that can help to improve balance, which you can do almost anywhere. I encourage you to choose one or two exercises that feel best for you and practice two to three times per week to enhance your balance and body awareness.

Glute bridges

Lie on a firm surface. Bend your knees and place the soles of your feet flat against the floor. Cross your arms over your chest and then lift your hips up off this surface as high as possible (you may need to use one hand for support at first). Hold for 3–5 seconds before lowering back down onto this same hard, flat ground. Do 20 repetitions per day.

Crab walk

Stand sideways with your feet shoulder-width apart to begin with. Take a step out with your left leg, then step your right leg towards your left, bringing yourself back to shoulder-width standing position. Practice on your left side 10–15 times a day, then swap to your right side the following day.

Balancing on one foot

Begin standing with your feet shoulder-width apart. Choose either your left or right leg to begin with. Stand on your chosen foot, trying to remain steady for as long as you can. Repeat on the opposite foot. Stand near a bench or doorway so that you have something to grab on to if you lose your balance or feel unsteady. Repeat five times on each foot.

RECLAIMING YOUR BODY THROUGH MINDFUL ATTENTION

You may have heard of mindfulness meditation, a type of stress-reduction technique that involves focusing on your breathing while allowing thoughts to come and go without judgment.

Body scan meditation is similar: you focus attention on different parts of your body and feel the sensations associated with them—such as warmth or coldness.

A progressive body scan meditation guides you to tune into your whole body, part by part, and notice how it feels by mentally scanning from the tips of your toes, all the way up to the crown of your head in a slow and intentional progression.

By consciously connecting with your body, you develop a deep awareness of all the different physical sensations and often how they connect with your emotions.

Learning to recognize parts of your body that you may be holding tension in can give you clarity and insight into your thoughts and feelings, but also allow you to consciously release and relax your muscles and joints.

This practice of tuning and checking in with your body can lead to improved mental, physical and emotional health as you deepen your awareness of your body and the connected emotional states that come with sensations.

Progressive body scan

This exercise is about noticing and experiencing your body. Some relaxation of your muscles may occur as you do this, but it's not necessary for the exercise to work properly.

Usually, our response to bodily pain or discomfort is to distract ourselves from it or try to numb the experience. In this exercise you will accept and notice with gentle curiosity your body in its comfort and discomfort—much like watching clouds move slowly across a blue sky on a sunny day.

Find a position that is both comfortable and relaxing, such as sitting or lying down. Unwind any tight clothing from around your waist.

Begin by focusing your attention on the physical sensations in your feet. What do they feel like? Is there any pain or discomfort, coolness or warmth? Whatever is present, notice it and be aware of those feelings without judging them as good or bad.

Now, allow your awareness to drift up from your feet,

through the rest of your lower legs—simply paying attention to any physical sensations in those parts.

Continue to gently move your awareness and attention further up your body, noticing each part of your physical self—your upper legs, hips, stomach, lower back, upper back, chest, hands, lower arms, upper arms and shoulders, neck, head, forehead, temples, eyes, cheeks, nose and mouth.

Once you have moved through all parts of your body, allow your attention to gently move down your body, noticing any places where you may still be feeling tension, pain or discomfort.

Remember, you are not trying to change your sensations or experiences, just simply register and become aware of them. Continue moving down your body until your awareness reaches back to your feet.

This exercise can take as little or as long as you desire. The more you lean into this practice and become more comfortable noticing bodily sensations and feelings, the more you can gradually increase the time spent in practice.

Your thoughts will always pop up during this exercise, and that's okay; we simply want to think and notice the thought and then, when you can, bring your awareness back to the body part you were focusing on previously.

RECLAIMING YOUR BODY THROUGH SOMATIC RELEASE

When we are in danger, threatened or fearful, our bodies release stress hormones such as cortisol and adrenaline. These stress hormones flood our bodies to prepare us to overcome the danger we face.

This is the fight-or-flight response (see page 19), and one of the most common experiences when we enter into this sympathetic state is to shake and tremble. (This is known as neurogenic tremors.)

We can use this shaking to our advantage to invoke neurogenic tremors. This allows the body to release chronic tension held within our muscles and bodies.

How to practice shaking

1. Sit against a wall as though you were sitting on a chair, with your back straight and feet spread comfortably apart.

2. Hold this position for as long as possible, until you reach the edge of your comfort zone. When you start to feel uncomfortable, move slightly up or down the wall.

3. Continue holding this position until it becomes too uncomfortable once more. Move your body up the wall slightly.

4. The aim of this exercise is to allow your legs to tremble/ tremor and shake without pain.

5. After about 3–5 minutes, rise from the wall into a standing position.

6. Bend your knees slightly and allow yourself to lean
    forward. It is normal for the body to tremble in this
    position; you may want to place your hands on the
    ground in order not to lose balance.

7. Allow yourself to hang, continuing to shake in this
    position until the shaking naturally comes to a stop, or
    hold for a minute before coming slowly back up to a
    standing position.

HOW TO INTEGRATE THE PRACTICES

Congratulations on completing Phase Two! In this part of the
process, you explored more deeply your relationship with and
understanding of your body—and continued strengthening the
foundation that you laid for yourself in Phase One.

In Phase Two, you learned how to expand your awareness
of your body and use it as a resource for emotional healing
through movement and balance exercises. You also learned
how to use your physical form for effective emotional release
and restoration.

The new practices and resources that you have learned in
Phase Two do not replace the resources from Phase One, but
instead complement them.

Again, integration of these practices is vital, but before we
look at the practices from Phase Two, let's do a quick audit and
clean-up of your Phase One practices.

Reflect on the following:

- Do any practices I have chosen from Phase One feel like they are being "forced" (aka not flowing or feeling good)?
- If yes, are there any practices from Phase One that I would like to change?
- Having practiced these resources for a period of time, do I need to make any functional changes to the order in which I complete certain practices?

Once you have completed your audit and made any necessary changes, let's look at how you can integrate these new practices into your day-to-day life. The practices in bold are Phase Two practices that you will be introducing.

Daily practices
- Daily Mood Record (night)
- Containment exercise (choose one)
- Body exercises (bee breathing or arm swings—daily)
- Regulating resources (one)
    - proprioceptive
    - cold exposure
    - singing
    - natural light
    - relaxing music
    - hot shower or bath
- **Gentle movement (choose one—practice every second or third day)**
    - swaying

- ° rocking
- ° swinging
- ° restorative yoga
- **Balance exercise (choose one—practice every second or third day)**
  - ° glute bridges
  - ° crab walk
  - ° balancing on one foot

One-off practice (but revisited intermittently)

- Nourishing your basic needs journal exercise (create action items)
- Mapping your nervous system (write down list of glimmers and keep handy)

Practices for when needed/desired

- **Somatic release—shaking**
- **Progressive body scan**
- Worry Record
- Recognizing and sitting with emotions
- Hyperarousal regulating resources (choose one)
  - ° proprioceptive
  - ° cold exposure
  - ° singing
- Hypoarousal (choose one)
  - ° natural light
  - ° relaxing music
  - ° hot shower or bath

Again, this is just a sample outline of how these practices could integrate into your daily life. The process of expansion and integration is highly unique, so you may find that certain tools are naturally no longer required as you introduce other new practices.

For example, one of the body exercises from Phase One was "arm swings." If you chose arm swings in Phase One, then you may notice that arm swings are very similar to the gentle action of swinging, which means that you wouldn't practice arm swings and swinging separately, but instead allow swinging to replace the previous practice of arm swings.

Follow your own intuitive nudges about what feels best for you and when you're ready to let go of certain practices.

It's also important that, as you move through these phases and beyond, these practices don't just disappear once you stop practicing them. They are always available to you whenever you need them. They continue to build out your personal library of regulating resources.

I encourage you to keep a list of your practices and resources, so that you always have something to come back to when you need it most.

Remember, repetition and consistency will allow you to integrate these practices into your life, creating a solid daily structure and ritual for you to nurture your nervous system and expand your personal resilience. Give yourself some time to implement and integrate before moving forwards into Phase Three too quickly.

8.
PHASE THREE: USING YOUR SUPERPOWER

THE ART OF LOVE IS LARGELY THE ART OF
PERSISTENCE.

Albert Ellis

Persistence, my friend, is an act of love, and you have continued to show up for yourself throughout Phases One and Two, and that is no small feat.

You have shown yourself radical self-love and acceptance by taking on the challenge of understanding and nurturing your mind, body and nervous system. For that, you should be incredibly proud of yourself and all of the work that you have done up to this point.

Together, we have created a secure base and built the ground under our feet to create a safe and sturdy foundation for us to stand on. We have used that solid foundation to then explore and reconnect with our bodies on a new and meaningful level, deepening our relationship to all the sensations and experiences that our bodies hold within their walls.

As you step into the third phase, you are ready to expand. In this phase you are going to be building resilience into your nervous system through expanding your parasympathetic nervous system via your vagus nerve (see page 29).

Phase Three is not a phase in the true sense—it's the ongoing nurturance and support of your body and mind as one. The practices throughout Phases One, Two and Three are the invisible safety net that hold massive space for you to grow, transition and navigate life on your own terms, feeling at home in your body and owning who you are to your core.

As you know by now, these phases are not linear—they are dynamic; they flow in tune with your life, allowing you to move through each and every moment, armed with an arsenal of tools that honor you, your needs and your experiences in all their diverse glory.

You already have so much to be proud of. You have given yourself the love and attention you truly deserve, maybe that you were never given in times of need. But here, in this moment, you are now able to confidently and boldly show the world that you are not defined by what has happened in your past, you are not defined by other people or things, you are not even defined by your emotions. Instead, you are defined by your innate capacity to just be uniquely you—and, by moving through these phases, you are learning who that truly is.

You are exploring the depth of wisdom that your body holds. You are recognizing that you are more than capable, when armed with the right tools and guidance, to share who you are with the world and ride the waves of life, no matter where they take you.

By the end of this phase, you will be armed with the necessary tools that give you back your power, sense of control and sense of self. I'm excited for you to take your next leap of discovery and understanding, so let's not delay any further!

PHASE THREE GROWTH

- The vagus nerve: your ally in conquering stress

- Heart rate variability

- Resetting your vagus nerve through healing movement

- Mindful movement and exercise

- Resetting your vagus nerve through lifestyle changes

- Resetting your vagus nerve through reconnective practices

THE VAGUS NERVE: YOUR ALLY IN CONQUERING STRESS

I'm going to let you in on a secret: you actually have super-powers. Yup! It's true. You, my friend, have superpowers. Maybe not the type that let you fly or turn invisible, but there's something just as amazing within your own body—your vagus nerve.

We first met the vagus nerve in Chapter 1, where we learned about its many functions, like regulating your heart rate and breathing, but we're going to revisit it together now, because this nerve is your secret weapon, your ally and your internal superpower. It protects you from panic attacks as well as chronic stress and anxiety by regulating your fight-or-flight response, and also has the capacity to make you more resilient to stress.

Remember, a regulated nervous system is a resilient nervous system (see Chapter 3), and our vagus nerve gives us the tools to build resilience into our nervous systems.

When you stimulate your vagus nerve, you feel calmer, your mood lifts, you feel more connected to others and have a clearer mind. Stimulating the vagus nerve also means that you increase your vagal tone—the measurement of activity of the vagus nerve and ultimately the parasympathetic nervous system (see page 29).

Increased vagal tone means that you feel more in control of your emotions, you foster deeper connections with others and your physical health improves too. You become more resilient and able to handle the challenges that life throws at you, and you increase your capacity to bounce back and even thrive after trauma, stress or big life events.

Putting in the work to support and nurture your vagus nerve means that you're going to be able to make healthier decisions for yourself, which in turn creates a ripple effect to all those around you.

Let's do a quick recap of the mighty vagus nerve.

It begins in our brain stem and runs down the left and right sides of our bodies, connecting our organs to our brains. The vagus nerve is an essential communication pathway between the brain and the body, and the body to the brain. Without it we wouldn't be able to breathe or digest our food properly. And guess what? Only mammals have this nerve!

Not only does your vagus nerve support vital functions like heart rate and breathing, but it also plays a major role in supporting the immune system and fighting inflammation.

The vagus nerve system acts to counterbalance the fight-or-flight response, triggering a relaxation response in our body.

HEART RATE VARIABILITY

We also met HRV in Chapter 1 (see page 24). Developing your HRV is one of the main goals of this phase of the program, but you don't have to buy expensive devices in order to begin to train your body and nervous system to increase your HRV.

We can use a simpler technique to gain valuable feedback on the functioning of our nervous system through tracking our heart rate consistently over a period of time.

While monitoring your heart rate is not giving you the direct measurement of your HRV, the daily practice of pausing and checking your current heart rate allows you to keep track of your progress in a meaningful, measurable and tangible way. As your nervous system expands and your vagus nerve strengthens, your heart rate will naturally begin to slow down.

This is what we want to track: how your resting heart rate changes over a period of time. It's not going to drastically lower overnight, but with repetition and practice, your resting heart rate may reduce, even just slightly—a sign that your vagal tone is increasing!

How to measure your heart rate

1.   Bring your attention to the pads of your pointer (index) and middle fingers (either left or right hand: your choice).

2.   With these two fingers, you're going to find your pulse, and you can try either your opposite wrist or your neck:

     Wrist: lightly press your index and middle fingers just below the base of the thumb (your middle fingers will just about cover the crease of your wrist).

     Neck: lightly press your index and middle fingers just below the angle of your jawbone.

3.   Once you have chosen an area of the body and can feel your pulse, use a stopwatch, clock with a second hand or timer and count the number of beats in 15 seconds.

4.   Multiply that number by four to find your heart rate.

You may want to repeat this practice three times to get the most accurate measurement. You can add up all three of your heart rate scores and then divide them by three in order to find the average reading.

Now that you have this information, we want to record the measurement. You can do this on a note in your phone, in a diary or notebook—it's not important where or how you track your heart rate, but it is important that you *do* track it.

I encourage you to measure your heart rate each morning upon waking. You can keep a diary/notepad next to your bed, measure your heart rate and just note down the date and number before starting your day. Remember, if you have any concerns about your heart rate see a doctor immediately.

This practice of record-keeping and tracking your daily experience in an objective way is going to allow you to gain valuable insight into the state of your nervous system, the health of your sleep, the impact of different stressors or triggers as well as the progress you are making in increasing your HRV over time with the practices in this phase.

Just while we're on the topic of record-keeping, think all the way back to Phase One—this is where you began your practice of daily worry and mood record-keeping (see pages 111 and 114). That ritual of reflection that you have already integrated into your daily practice runs alongside this new information that you are gaining through recording and tracking your heart rate.

By remaining consistent, you get a clear understanding of how your day-to-day physiological and emotional experiences—and insight from your heart rate—impact one another.

This is where the rubber meets the road. You are moving from knowledge, to experience and back into knowledge! You will begin to notice how certain triggers affect your heart rate, as well as what patterns and cues spark changes in your ANS. Not only will you notice when triggers or stressors impact your nervous system, but you will also be able to refine the tools and resources that you are practicing to positively support your vagus nerve and nervous system.

HRV training is an integrative practice. It allows you to effectively map out your day-to-day experiences, gain insight from these and make informed changes where necessary.

As you continue through this phase, it's vital that you continue tracking your daily experiences and moods—not just your heart rate score!

But how do you actually increase vagal tone? And is it even possible?

The answer is yes! It can be done, but it's important to understand that, like all of the practices, processes and journeys that are involved in healing, increasing your HRV and decreasing your resting heart rate takes time. Your time frame is unique to you, and results do not happen overnight.

Instead of focusing too much on the numbers, turn your focus into creating rituals—new patterns that hold space for your nervous system, body and mind to expand into. Remember, whatever is familiar is most safe to your nervous system, so repetition and consistency over long periods of time teach your nervous system a new version of safety.

In this phase you are going to be exposed to and learn many different practices, including gentle lifestyle shifts—some of them may not resonate with you; some of them may feel really damn good for you. Explore, experiment and listen to the intuitive nudge that your nervous system is sending to you. Don't be afraid to try something and dislike it—this is the core of deepening and honoring your beautiful individuality. It's all just feedback that you are receiving from your wise body and is never a negative reflection of you as a human.

Together we are going to explore integrative practices, and there is no better place to begin this journey into resetting your vagus nerve than with healing movement.

RESETTING YOUR VAGUS NERVE THROUGH HEALING MOVEMENT

Now that you've revisited how incredible your vagus nerve is and the ways in which you can measure your vagal tone, it's time to activate your vagus nerve and increase your vagal tone through healing movement.

A key part of this is learning how to use movement as a way to reset your nervous system when it's become overstimulated or overwhelmed by stressors.

The advantages of learning how to use movement as a tool for self-regulation are vast. Movement can help us manage our emotions and thoughts more effectively; it can reduce stress and anxiety over time; and it can increase our capacity to deal with life's challenges in a more positive way by increasing our vagal tone.

Movement also helps us to regulate our internal states more effectively through increasing stress tolerance and resilience within your nervous system. This means that you will be less reactive and more flexible when faced with challenges or stressors in your life.

Not only does movement increase our resilience and stress tolerance, but it also creates space for the body and mind to release unprocessed emotions and experiences. Our bodies are hardwired to move, and movement is an innate form of self-regulation. When we don't allow our bodies to move freely or often enough, we allow ourselves to become more vulnerable to stress and anxiety.

Movement is also a powerful way to connect with your body and mind. It helps you feel more grounded in your physical experience, which can help regulate your emotions and thoughts more effectively. When we are able to feel the sensations of our bodies moving freely through space, we often experience a sense of ease or flow that allows us to let go of stress and anxiety.

Somatic movement is being aware and present in your body as you move in different ways, and being able to connect with the sensations occurring internally while being aware of your interaction with the environment around you.

Somatic movement, or movement-based approaches to awareness of the body and its environment can be thought of as involving three aspects:

1. **Interoception:** the perception of internal sensations.

2. **Exteroception:** the perception of the external environment.

3. **Proprioception:** perceiving and sensing your movement within a physical space.

Throughout the following somatic movement practices, make it your intention to shift your focus to your internal experience of a movement. Somatic movements are not designed to be aesthetically pleasing and neither are they about trying to force your body to move in ways that it does not want to. Instead, it's using the internal experience and feedback of your body to guide your movements.

As you build out and integrate somatic movement into your day-to-day life, you may also notice that your emotional awareness gently increases too. Physical flow offers a space to process, release and experience difficult emotions in a non-verbal capacity. It allows emotions to be felt and offers new patterns and creative ways for your nervous system to downregulate through an expressive and visceral practice, rather than having to cognitively work and talk through them.

The exercises below are you opening the door to further exploration. You are encouraged to explore each movement with an open mind and, if you find that one in particular resonates more with you, let that be a gentle nudge to explore that type of action further.

Somatic stretching

Somatic stretches are based on pandiculation, a physiological process in which muscles contract and relax regularly. An example of this is the way we tend to stretch when waking up from sleep.

The pandicular response is a natural process that our nervous system uses to release muscle tension. Somatic stretching is designed to imitate this same release of muscle tension.

Somatic stretching emphasizes learning to feel the tension held in our muscles and fascia rather than ignoring it. While this practice appears under the heading of healing movement, it generally requires more stillness than physical action.

Being motionless allows space for the nervous system and brain to slow down enough so you actually tap into the undercurrent of sensation occurring within your body, reconnecting with the sensory experience of just being within your own body. By reconnecting with these sensory experiences, we can enhance our awareness and connection with our own body. This experience of inner connection aligns perfectly with polyvagal theory, which underlines how our nervous system affects our ability to connect with ourselves and the world around us (see Chapter 1).

The following are three simple somatic stretching exercises for you to explore.

Standing awareness

A wonderful way to get a feel for your body is simply standing still and paying attention to various muscles as you breathe.

Tuning into your body, the sensations and different muscle groups can take time. This gentle somatic stretch builds your body awareness before taking the next step in somatic stretching.

1. Stand up straight with your feet firmly planted on the floor, and notice how this stance makes you feel grounded.

2. Scrunch or spread your toes to feel the connection between your feet and the ground.

3. Try tightening and releasing your foot muscles for one minute.

4. Bring your attention to your breath. Inhale through your
    nose for a count of 5–7 seconds. Notice the expansion of
    your abdominal muscles as you inhale.

5. Exhale gently through pursed lips, noticing your muscles
    in your abdominals contracting.

6. Repeat this slow inhale and gentle exhalation ten times,
    each time noticing the expansion and contraction of
    muscles, as well as any sensations in your body.

7. Once you're finished, remain standing and take a moment
    to scan your body from head to toe. Notice how different
    muscle groups feel, notice if there are any muscles that feel
    tense and notice any muscles that feel relaxed.

Gentle back and abdominal stretch

The following somatic stretch is also referred to as a glute bridge.
In Phase Two, we explored this exercise for its role in building
balance (see page 172). Now we are revisiting it as a somatic
stretch because it allows you to release tension and then regain
control of the muscles in your lower back and abdominals, which
can be helpful if you're experiencing back pain.

This is a low-impact exercise that you can do while lying
down.

1. Lying down, place your feet flat on the floor, with your
    knees bent at hip-distance apart.

2. Breathe deeply, paying attention to the muscles in your back and abdomen as they move.

3. Slowly arch your back, pressing your belly upwards towards the ceiling and pushing into the floor with both feet, activating your glute muscles.

4. You can remain in this position for as long as feels comfortable. Then, when you're ready to come out of it, slowly lower your back until it's flat on the floor.

5. As you do the movement, look for any places of tension and try to relax those muscles.

6. Repeat 3–5 times, with a long rest in between each exercise.

Iliopsoas stretch

The iliopsoas is a group of muscles that connects the spine to the legs. Many people hold at least some tension in this muscle group, especially those who have desk jobs or otherwise spend lots of time sitting down.

This somatic stretch allows you to bring gentle awareness to this muscle group as well as the surrounding muscles, and gently releases tension.

1. Lying down, place your feet flat on the floor with your knees bent at hip-distance apart.

2. Bring your right hand behind your head, allowing your head to be cradled in the palm of your hand.

3. Slowly lift your head gently with your right hand as you simultaneously lift your right leg (knee bent) approximately 6 inches off the floor (your left side will remain on the ground).

4. Focus your attention on the muscles in your lower back, hips and legs. Notice how they feel. Notice any tension in this area.

5. Hold this position for as long as is comfortable. Then slowly lower your head and leg at the same time.

6. Pause on the ground for 30 seconds, breathing deeply and just noticing the sensations in your body.

7. When you are ready, repeat on the same side, only this time, straighten your right leg as you lift.

8. Repeat this pattern 3–5 times on your right side, before changing to your left.

9. Hold each position for as long as is comfortable, with 30 seconds or more in between movements.

If you found these somatic stretching exercises helpful, try practicing each stretch for five minutes a day. Over time and with consistent practice, your awareness of the sensation in your body will increase—and so will muscle relaxation.

MINDFUL MOVEMENT AND EXERCISE

Movement, in whatever form it takes—from dancing to walking around the block—can be a healing experience.

As you move your body, you tap into a natural healing system that can help you to release stress and anxiety. You may find that some activities are more soothing than others, and there is no right or wrong way to experience this process. The key is to find a movement that allows you to reconnect with your body and move in a way that feels good and actually interests you—something that gets you excited!

As I explained in Chapter 4, for me, that was mixed martial arts. I loved every facet of the sport—the smell of the gym, my training partners who turned into friends, the way in which my muscles burned and my body and brain dipped into a flow state when I was training.

For you it will be a completely unique experience. Maybe you already have an idea as to what type of movement feels good or maybe you are unsure—both still hold space for deeper exploration into yourself, your desires, preferences, lifestyle and the current state of your nervous system.

Exercise and mindful movement are tools that can effectively improve and increase your vagal tone. They're also highly accessible, with many forms of exercise and mindful movement that can be done in the comfort of your own home.

On top of increasing vagal tone, exercise and mindful movement provide an avenue of release. Your nervous system and body are designed to move—from the moment you are born until this point right now in your life, movement plays an integral role in your every day.

Movement is a highly functional and useful resource for us with additional holistic health benefits like:

- supporting a healthy brain
- managing weight
- strengthening bones and muscles
- reducing the risk of disease in the long term
- improving our ability to complete day-to-day tasks

Sympathetic activation is needed when we move our bodies due to the increase of energy expenditure. We want our sympathetic nervous system to be online when we are exerting energy so that we can get more blood to our muscles and organs (see page 19). This is why, when we are out of breath, we often find ourselves breathing through our mouths—to increase the volume of oxygen circulating in our bodies.

You might be thinking right now, *I want to lower my sympathetic activation, not increase it!* And you are right: the overall goal is to decrease sympathetic activation and increase the strength of your vagal tone and ventral vagal nervous system. In order to do that, gentle exposure to physiological stress, for example through exercise and mindful movement, is necessary for the nervous system to become resilient and downregulate the sympathetic response.

Your sympathetic nervous system is not the bad guy: you need it in order to not only survive, but also any time you need to expend more energy than you would in a state of rest. Think about the last time you had to run to get home, catch the train, bus or plane or even to your car because you were late or stuck in a downpour of rain. Or even think back to the last time you felt really excited and energetic! These are all examples of when your sympathetic nervous system was helpful.

Exercise and mindful movement activates your sympathetic nervous system and puts your body under physiological "stress"—allowing you to exert more energy and use up sugar stores in the body. When we do this consistently over a period of time, our tolerance builds up. What felt hard when you first started doing it, now feels a lot easier. For example, you may have started running—on that first run your lungs and muscles were probably burning and you couldn't run that far. But as you continued to practice, you're now running double or triple the distance you did in the beginning before you hit that wall.

So exercise and mindful movement expand your tolerance towards physiological stress. They also expand the capacity of certain physiological functions like breathing, muscle and bone density, and cardiovascular efficiency. These systems are now functioning at a higher level and capacity than they were previously, allowing for more efficient use of energy stores throughout the day when you're not exercising or moving your body in an energetic way.

Your nervous system becomes more resilient and tolerant from the repetitive exposure to physiological stress, decreasing sympathetic nervous system activity over time. Simultaneously, HRV increases, which means your vagal tone is strengthening, making it easier to access calmer states for longer periods of time and expanding your capacity to handle challenges that life throws at you.

You don't need to start training for a marathon or become a world-class weightlifter to reap the rewards of exercise and mindful movement. There is benefit in movement in any form, whatever that may look like for you. It's important to meet yourself where you're at. If exercise and mindful movement is not a practice that you currently have in your life, then starting small and exploring different types of exercise that you may enjoy will allow you to create a consistent practice.

Start small

A quick note about the importance of starting small—habits are formed over time, and generally need repetition and consistency. If movement is new, there is always going to be resistance because it has not yet been integrated into your practices. As humans, we also have a desire to "go big or go home," but when it comes to movement, this can be counterproductive.

Any new forms of movement are going to be felt through-out your body. Muscles that you didn't even know existed are going to be used for the first time in a long while and, if you go too hard, your body is going to struggle to recover effectively. The longer it takes for your body to recover, the less likely you are to go back to that form of movement, at least not without a lot of internal resistance. Less is more, especially in the beginning of introducing mindful movement and exercise into your life.

More exercise is not necessarily better. Over-exercising or too much high-intensity movement without enough recovery time actually lowers HRV.

Like so many activities, there is a point of diminishing return. A good example is if you decide to go for a long run when you haven't run in years: you might get through the exercise, but then every single muscle in your body aches for weeks afterwards, discouraging you from even thinking about going for another run anytime soon. Seeing results is motivating, which is why we want to start small—and experience some wins without overwhelming our body and mind—then slowly build up and expand our nervous system, muscles and respiratory and cardiovascular systems in the process. Listen to your body, drop in to notice any tension or resistance, tune into when your body's saying "yes" and when it is saying "no" to being pushed.

Consistency is key

Another important aspect of harnessing the benefits of exercise and mindful movement is consistency. I've mentioned repetition and consistency a few times now, and I want to clear a few things up.

Quite often when we hear the word "consistent," our brains jump to "I have to do this every day"—which is not necessarily true. To be consistent merely means to do something (act in a certain way, carry out certain behaviors, and so on) over a period of time. There is no mention that you have to do that behavior or action every single day, just that it is performed regularly over a period of time.

This is where many people get tripped up. We have the expectation of ourselves to be able to do something from the minute we decide and then continue doing that thing every single day. If you've ever tried to create a new habit, you know that it is a highly unrealistic expectation to have of ourselves. Sometimes we forget, sometimes we get sick, sometimes we are tired, often other things in our life take priority for a while. This is normal.

So let's reframe consistency to be something far more realistic and achievable. Consistency is whatever makes sense for you and your day-to-day life. It has to make sense when and how you put aside time to exercise or move your body. For you, there may only be one day a week when you could realistically start exercising in a way that feels good for you. For someone else, that could be two or three times scattered throughout the week.

Consistency is not about how many times you get to do something, but that you do that thing regularly for a while. Whether that's once a week over the course of a few months/years or every day, both are consistent.

Another aspect of consistency is also being realistic with the amount of time and energy you have to complete the task. Remember, starting small will allow you to build up your HRV.

If you decide that you are going to exercise twice a week for one hour, but then something happens and you don't have a full hour to complete your session, then you start to fall out of consistency. But if you start small—for example with only five minutes of exercise and movement—then you create so much more space for you to be successful and consistent.

The more success you experience when integrating a new habit or practice, the more likely you are to come back to it—dopamine, the neurotransmitter involved with motivation and reward, plays a big role in this process.

Because mindful movement and exercise are so diverse, we aren't going to look at specific exercises, but instead I've offered some examples for inspiration.

Endurance exercises

Endurance or aerobic exercise is geared towards increasing your breathing and heart rate above 50 percent of your baseline maximum while you are performing it.

Examples of endurance exercises include:

- brisk walking
- jogging/running
- dancing
- swimming
- cycling
- hiking or climbing stairs
- playing sports like football, tennis or basketball

Strength exercises

Strength or resistance exercise is a type of anaerobic activity that makes muscles stronger by working against a weight or force.

Examples of strength exercises include:

- body-weight exercises like push-ups, sit-ups and squats
- free weights using kettlebells, dumbbells and barbells

- everyday activities like carrying groceries
- resistance-band exercises

Balance exercises

Balance is the ability to control your body's center of gravity within the limits established by your base of support (the points at which you make contact with whatever surface you are standing on).

Body balance is a complex process that involves many of the body's systems, including the vestibular and proprioceptive sensory systems (see pages 159 and 145).

Examples of balance exercises include:

- tai chi or yoga
- balancing on one foot and lifting the other foot off the ground
- heel-to-toe walking
- getting up and sitting down from a chair without the help of your hands

RESETTING YOUR VAGUS NERVE THROUGH LIFESTYLE CHANGES

The idea of "lifestyle changes" doesn't normally evoke a sense of excitement among people and, because of that, they are often overlooked in the grand scheme of our health and well-being. But even if you haven't been aware of it, what you have been doing throughout the phase work of this book when you implement a new practice or ritual is applying lifestyle changes.

Essentially, lifestyle changes are shifts or alterations you make in your behavior or habits in your day-to-day life that create positive change or growth.

Some common examples of lifestyle changes include:

- healthy sleeping patterns
- eating nutritious foods
- moving or exercising your body
- relaxation practices
- drinking enough water each day

Take another look at that list of common lifestyle changes—most of these are habits that we do without even thinking about them anymore—we tend to repeat something for long enough so that we can then put it on autopilot and not have to expend any more energy than necessary. But oftentimes, because many lifestyle practices are running on autopilot or have just become so normalized, we tend not to take into account how they may be impacting us on a physiological level.

Lifestyle changes tend to be the most tricky to implement, simply because they are so ingrained. There is usually some level of subconscious resistance when it comes to making change. This is because, while your brain is amazing, it's incredibly lazy. It loves to create patterns that it can repeat over and over until it's like a shortcut and you don't have to cognitively think about doing that action or behavior anymore. For example, you don't have to think about brushing your teeth—if you had to think about each step every single morning and evening, it would be pretty exhausting.

It's important to be mindful of this when looking at any form of lifestyle changes—like implementing new types of consistent exercise or movement—and start small.

It's not recommended to try to change absolutely everything at the same time. Too much change too soon is completely overwhelming to your nervous system and, instead of these shifts having a positive effect, they will only push you further into a survival state.

Below I am going to share a number of lifestyle changes—you do not have to do all of them to get positive results. In fact, you are encouraged to only start with one small alteration and practice, practice, practice.

After a period of time, this new habit becomes integrated—you don't have to think about doing it, you just will! That's the point at which you are ready to take on another small change.

The lifestyle adjustments that we are going to look at below are ones that can move the needle most effectively and quickly for many people. These small changes in your life have the ability to increase HRV, strengthen vagal tone, build resilience into your nervous system and downregulate an overactive sympathetic or dorsal vagal response.

These may feel too simple or "not enough" but trust me, if you commit to making even just one of these lifestyle changes the new normal in your own day-to-day, you will not only support your vagus nerve and nervous system, but you will begin to regain your energy and confidence in your body's ability to heal and restore.

Lifestyle change #1: sleep

Sleep deprivation and insomnia are no strangers to me. From the ages of 16 to 21 years old, I suffered from chronic and ongoing sleep issues. The night became my enemy: I would toss and turn until the early hours of the morning, only to drag myself out of bed to go to school. I found myself falling asleep in my chair in the middle of classes, and I could barely hold my focus for more than a few minutes before my mind drifted off.

In the beginning, the frustration was overwhelming. I would often find myself so exhausted that all I could do was cry. My body felt weaker and weaker over time, and I found myself becoming more and more isolated from the "day people."

I couldn't connect with others in a meaningful way because my brain felt like it was always on the verge of tipping into a dark abyss that I wasn't sure I'd be able to pull myself out of.

As time passed, I somehow just accepted this new normal of sleepwalking through the day and spending the nights with my dark thoughts. It was the type of tiredness that makes you want to give up everything in life.

In a way, I had given up on life and my existence became increasingly small. I didn't have the energy to do many of the things that I would have liked to do as a teenager and young adult. It was a strange juxtaposition to live in a sleepwalking state with no one even knowing. Because despite how dark my thoughts became, how long the nights felt or how removed I made myself, I still had a foot in the door with the external world. I worked and studied, occasionally saw friends and would go out (a lot).

But ultimately it felt like my life had become a constant race to get home, to return to my bedroom. Even though my bedroom was the one place that I couldn't get the thing I needed most—proper sleep—it became my sanctuary.

My experience with insomnia and sleep deprivation isn't unique. As many as 40 percent of the population worldwide suffers from sleep deprivation or insufficient sleep duration for various reasons, including night-shift work, lifestyle choices, insomnia as well as trauma and PTSD.

Sleep may appear to be a simple process yet, as a society, we often overlook how crucial for optimal health and well-being it truly is.

The quality of your sleep directly impacts your brain's ability to regulate hormones, emotions and cardiovascular function. It is a powerful tool for restoring and resetting your nervous system. When you sleep, your body is able to repair any damage done during the day while you are awake, including restorative processes related to inflammation. It's also one of the most important tools for increasing HRV and supporting healthy vagal tone.

Lack of sleep comes with a whole host of negative side effects such as:

- increased levels of inflammation
- increased risk of cardiovascular disease, type 2 diabetes and gastrointestinal disorders
- heightened stress response
- increased pain
- depression

- anxiety
- cognitive issues
- memory issues

When sleep is disrupted, our ANS can become unbalanced. This affects involuntary functions including temperature regulation, HRV, respiration, sexual arousal and bowel and bladder control.

As we learned in Chapter 2, the ANS allows the body to respond to internal and external stimuli by balancing the sympathetic and parasympathetic nervous system. When we begin to feel sleepy and drowsy, the parasympathetic nervous system is activated as our vagus nerve's electrical activity increases (vagal tone). Our heart rate slows down and blood pressure decreases as we move from non-rapid eye movement (NREM) sleep into deeper stages.

During sleep, we go through different stages of NREM and REM (rapid eye movement) sleep. During the NREM stages, our parasympathetic nervous system is more active; during the REM stage, when dreaming occurs, our sympathetic nervous system dominates.

When we are under stress, our sympathetic nervous system is more activated than usual. This means the parasympathetic nervous system does not come online making it difficult to prepare the body for sleep as heart rate remains high.

The vagus nerve plays a crucial role in sleep and sleep plays a crucial role in creating and maintaining healthy vagal tone. Sleep deprivation has been shown to increase heart rate from baseline measurements, compared to normal sleep conditions.

The increase in heart rate may well be due to a reduction in vagal tone.

Good quality sleep increases vagal tone and HRV, promoting further healthy sleep patterns. Lack of sleep decreases vagal tone and HRV, causing more difficulty falling asleep and creating a frustrating nightly cycle. In order to break that pattern, you can begin to proactively increase your vagal tone and HRV. We're going to look at simple and effective ways that you can begin to do just that in a moment.

Sleep is a lifestyle change that requires conscious attention to what and how we are doing things during the day. It is also one of the more challenging lifestyle changes to nail. It takes time, sometimes a frustratingly long time, to bring your sleep back into a healthy pattern. However, if you persist with your sleep, you will be rewarded tenfold with energy, emotional regulation and a greater capacity to handle day-to-day challenges. Don't give up on your sleep.

Okay, I think you're ready to tackle the sleep monster and reclaim truly restorative rest. Let's have a look at some simple and effective ways that you can do just that.

Resonant breath training for better sleep

As a society, we chronically overbreathe, with most people taking between 12 and 16 breaths per minute. Your rate of breathing may not have been something that you consciously tuned into before, because this rhythmic function happens automatically. But what if I told you that your breath is actually the fastest and most effective way to balance your ANS and increase vagal tone? Slow, rhythmic diaphragmatic breathing can enhance the tone of your vagus nerve and increase your HRV.

Studies have found that the optimal breathing rate for the nervous system and body is actually 6–10 breaths per minute. It's not only the rate of breathing that is important, but also *how* you breathe. Nasal breathing (through the nose) is also important in optimizing your breathing patterns.

Resonant breath training is a technique that slows down your breathing rate to approximately six breaths per minute, maximizing your HRV. This state can make you feel at ease and relaxed—and, if you're sleep-deprived, even sleepy.

To get the best results, think of this breathing technique more like training. You are training yourself to breathe correctly and optimizing your nervous system. In order to do that, practicing resonant breath at multiple points throughout your day will allow you to lower your baseline stress levels and begin to increase your vagal tone.

Correcting your breathing takes time, but as you begin to retrain your breath, you will be able to use this breathing technique to downregulate your nervous system whenever you may need to.

In order to practice resonant breathing, we need to first learn to activate and breathe with our diaphragms. When you are breathing with your diaphragm, your belly naturally expands when you inhale and contracts when you exhale.

This first step is often the hardest as many of us have been breathing incorrectly for most of our lives. Take a moment to pause and just notice *how* you're breathing right now:

- Place one hand on your chest and the other on your belly.
- Does your belly expand when you inhale? Or does your chest move when you inhale?

For many people, normal breathing looks like shallow breathing into the chest area. This is typical when we are doing a hard workout or under stress, because faster paced, shallow breathing allows more oxygen to enter the lungs. But chest breathing is not optimal for rest, relaxation or recovery.

Learning to breathe with your diaphragm is your first step. Here's how to do it:

- It's best to practice first lying down flat. Inhale through your nose and imagine your belly expanding like a balloon towards the ceiling.
- If you are struggling to get your belly to expand when you inhale, it can be helpful to apply light weight to the belly to help activate the diaphragm. You can place a book or heat pack on your belly, or just place both hands over your belly button.
- As you exhale, your stomach will deflate and contract towards the floor.
- Your chest should not be moving; just the belly expanding and contracting.
- Practice activating the diaphragm and expanding the belly as you inhale for five minutes per day for a week. You don't have to worry about the pace of your breathing—just train yourself to breathe with your diaphragm.

If after a week you are still finding it difficult to breathe with your diaphragm, continue practicing for another week before moving on to the next step.

Now that you're breathing with your diaphragm, we can start to shift the pace of your breathing. Six breaths per minute typically looks like:

- Five-second inhale, five-second exhale, or
- Four-second inhale, six-second exhale

Achieving six breaths per minute is the goal, but in the beginning, if you find your breathing rate is higher, that's okay. You want to gradually lower your breathing rate over time.

Practice slowing down your breathing rate (remembering to breathe with your diaphragm) for five minutes each day. Five minutes is all you need to start to retrain your breath for optimal vagal tone and HRV.

As you feel more comfortable with this slow, diaphragmatic breathing pattern, you can start to use it when lying in bed to promote healthy and restful sleep.

Lifestyle change #2: natural light

One of the best ways to support your vagus nerve and nervous system is by exposing yourself to natural light, preferably in the morning. This exposure helps regulate cortisol production, regulates melatonin levels and, most importantly, supports healthy circadian rhythms.

Your circadian rhythm is kind of like an inbuilt timetable that exists in every single cell in your body, including your brain.

This timetable sets the rhythm for functions like sleep, body temperature, metabolism and mood.

Circadian rhythm can fall out of timing, especially during times of stress and elevated cortisol levels. This can cause instability in the sleep–wake cycle, which runs on a 24-hour inbuilt clock.

Natural bright light affects your sleep and mood indirectly by regulating the availability of neurotransmitters such as serotonin, which plays a role in regulating our emotional state. It also guides and stabilizes circadian rhythms by synchronizing them with environmental time cues (sunrise and sunset).

Natural light is essentially a free, accessible and easy resource that can support your circadian rhythms and healthy sleep patterns, as well as stabilizing mood.

Natural light gives your body important cues to help reset your circadian rhythm, especially first thing in the morning. Exposure to natural light first thing in the morning helps your body to fall back in line with that internal timetable that is inbuilt in your cells.

Light is an important cue for your body's sleep cycle. The light you are exposed to during the day helps your body figure out when it's time to go to bed (and when it's time to wake up).

How to get more light

Exposing yourself to natural light first thing in the morning is when you will gain the most benefit. Ideally within the first hour after you wake up, you should be in direct natural light for about 20 plus minutes.

It's important to note that direct exposure—no sunglasses, hat or anything that filters light like windows—will maximize the benefits of natural light.

It's also equally necessary to understand that it does not have to be sunny or even a blue sky for you to benefit from natural light. If you live in a colder climate or it's overcast or raining, there is still natural light present that will regulate your circadian rhythm effectively. All you need to do is turn your face towards where the sun would be in the sky!

Lifestyle change #3: cold exposure

You have probably come across videos or images of people jumping into ice-cold pools or speaking about cold showers; it seems as though everyone is dipping their toe (pun intended) into the cold-water pool.

Cold thermogenesis, or cold exposure, is having its time in the spotlight and there's actually a very good reason why cold exposure has taken the world by storm.

Dunking your body into freezing cold water is not a new practice: humans have been doing this for centuries, and it turns out that cold exposure is one of the best ways to stimulate the vagus nerve, increasing vagal tone.

The latest research into cold exposure and cold thermo-genesis shows that regular routine exposure to cold water lowers sympathetic activation and increases the activity of the parasympathetic nervous system.

Not only does cold exposure strengthen your vagal tone, but it also provides many whole-body benefits such as:

- improved heart and lung function
- enhanced immune system
- modulation of inflammation
- regulation of the stress response

Cold exposure often sends people running for the hills, but you don't have to jump into an ice bath immediately and hit a world record to get the benefits. In fact, like all lifestyle changes, it's important to start small and gradually build up your tolerance over time.

Cold exposure can come in many forms—the key is to find a type of cold exposure that suits you and your needs.

Here are some examples of cold exposure that you can experiment with:

- having a cold shower at the end of your warm shower
- taking an ice bath
- submerging your head in cold water
- applying a cold compress to the sides of neck and chest
- spending time outside in cold temperatures

As you can see, there are much gentler ways to try out cold exposure, especially at the start of your journey. It's not a competition for who can be in an ice bath the longest—it's the process of honoring your current state and meeting yourself where you're at.

If that looks like starting off with a cold compress on your neck and chest, that's amazing! There's no wrong way or right way, just the way that works best for you.

RESETTING YOUR VAGUS NERVE THROUGH RECONNECTIVE PRACTICES

In today's world, many people view connection as something they want rather than need. This isn't surprising—during the Covid-19 pandemic we became physically isolated and disconnected from friends, family members and our community at large. The world shifted into the online space—and working from home, Zoom workout sessions and FaceTime have now become the norm for many.

Despite our increased ability to connect with people from all over the world through a few clicks of a button, there is now more than ever a deep sense of isolation and loneliness among many of those who lived through the pandemic.

Approximately 33 percent of adults experience loneliness globally—that is over a third of the population that feels as though they do not have access to genuine human connection with other people.

The truth is that humans are hardwired for connection. Feeling like you belong or having others to support you is fundamental to the human experience. It's not a luxury; it's necessary for our physiological and psychological well-being.

Humans evolved and developed the ability to form and maintain strong social bonds, which has had many benefits: reduced vulnerability to predators, greater access to food resources and protection from harassment. Social connection expanded humans' capacity to create physical safety and increase the chance for survival.

But social connection and relationships don't just offer physical safety, they also increase our ability to cope with stress more effectively. Strong social ties create a greater sense of predictability and control in our lives, boosting psychological and emotional safety.

Our social engagement system operates at its best when our environment feels safe and predictable. A strong social engagement system allows us to forge and build out a supportive network of people who can guide us through life's ups and downs, and motivate us to pursue our goals.

Oxytocin also plays an important role in this process. This is a hormone that supports feelings of love and trust, and can be released when we experience certain types of touch sensation, music, exercise and, most importantly, when we feel connected to someone. When oxytocin is released, it also increases HRV, which furthers our capacity to engage and feel present and connected with others.

Co-regulation

Some studies have found that couples in romantic relationships actually experience something called cardiac synchrony—where heart rate and HRV between two people match one another. It was also found that during moments where one member of the couple became dysregulated and their HRV dropped, the other member of the couple increased their HRV in order to help regulate their partner.

This all occurs on a subconscious level, but beautifully illustrates the physiological dance that occurs between humans—co-regulation. Essentially, co-regulation is a process that occurs through trusted connections, in which one individual may "borrow" from a regulated nervous system in order to self-regulate and bring themselves back to a ventral vagal (parasympathetic) state.

Humans co-regulate throughout their lifespan. As a baby, we rely on the gentle cues from our parents or caregivers in order to know that we are safe. As we grow into toddlers and adolescents, co-regulation remains vital in order to create safety, connection and build the ability and capacity to self-regulate through challenging or difficult emotions or stressful life experiences.

As adults, the need for co-regulation does not disappear, especially when we are experiencing chronic or ongoing stress, life changes and transitions or grief. The importance of having others who can create a sense of safety within us when we are not able to do this for ourselves gives us the ability to reach a state of grounded calm and we can then take over the self-regulation process ourselves.

Humans co-regulate through a number of different ways, such as:

- The eyes—eye "crinkles" around the edge of the eyes when someone is genuinely smiling, a soft or hard gaze.
- Head positioning—head tilts convey safety and empathy.
- Vocal prosody—the pace of speech as well as the intonation (soft, hard, musical, gentle, aggressive).
- Forward-leaning, open body posture.
- Gentle rhythmic sounds.

These physiological shifts and gestures can be thought of as your "cues of safety." You may remember the term "neuro-ception," which we explored on page 16. It is the process in which our ANS deciphers the world and understands whether the environment is safe or dangerous. It does this through receiving these physiological cues of safety from others. All of this often occurs on a subconscious level, but gestures can also be consciously used in order to support nervous system regulation.

Connection and social engagement with trusted and safe others are crucial and important pieces of the regulation puzzle. We can also use certain physiological shifts and cues of safety individually to support and maintain healthy vagal tone and activate our social engagement system in order to more easily connect with others.

Throughout all the phases within this book, we have looked at resources, techniques and tools that create a sense of safety and allow space for release and restoration within the nervous system. The reconnective practices you will be learning in a moment enhance your ability to connect with others and are like placing the roof on your dream home. They solidify the expansion that has taken place within your own physiology by enhancing your personal resilience and capacity to face challenges in your life.

Together, we are going to draw Phase Three to a close with two powerful reconnective practices that enhance co-regulation and social engagement.

Vocal prosody

Your voice is a very important part of being a human. It is one of the main pathways in which you are able to communicate and interact with the external world—sharing your thoughts, emotions, ideas, boundaries, needs and dreams. Your voice is also fundamentally important in conveying *who* you are and the experience that you are having from moment to moment (your emotions).

Prosody is the rhythm, tempo and tone of voice, and provides important information about someone that goes beyond just the words they are speaking. For example, if you have ever asked someone if they are okay, and the response was "I'm fine" but said in a blunt and monotone way, you might immediately realize that they are, in fact, not "fine."

The way in which the voice expresses gives you necessary insight into the current attitude or emotional state someone may be in. Our ears have evolved over time in a way to be able to detect and notice these tiny changes in tone of voice, rhythm and tempo, in order to figure out whether or not someone is safe or a potential threat (neuroception again).

Voices that have variation—they go up and down, kind of like a song—tend to be received as cues of safety when compared to voices that are monotone or lack variation, which can be interpreted as potentially threatening or dangerous. Interestingly, a common symptom of low vagal tone is impaired social communication, including monotone speech.

We can use vocal prosody when we are engaging with others by identifying and noticing *how* they are communicating and speaking to us in order to activate our own social engagement system. Some people in your life will have greater variation and vocal prosody and you can connect and notice these tiny shifts in the way they are communicating in order to shift into a ventral vagal state, co-regulate and connect on a deeper level with those individuals.

The muscles in your vocal cords are also all innervated by the vagus nerve—meaning that your voice is both a window into the current state of your vagus nerve, as well as being a tool to influence and enhance vagal tone to activate your social engagement system.

Pay attention to how you speak and practice changing your vocal prosody. You can do this in the safety of your own home, in front of a mirror. Speak out loud as if you were having a conversation with someone. Change the volume, tone and pitch of your voice from loud to whispering, musical to monotone. This will give you the opportunity to notice the way in which you are speaking with others, and create more opportunity to intentionally shift the tone of your voice or the rhythm and tempo in order to deepen your sense of safety and connection with others.

You can also use a combination of your breath and voice to activate your vagus nerve, in turn increasing your ability for enhanced vocal prosody.

Breath and vocal-toning practice

This simple practice activates your vocal cords, shifts the tone of your voice and elongates your exhale in order to gently activate the vagus nerve.

Here's how to do it:

1. Find a comfortable seated position, back straight and shoulders relaxed.

2. You can close your eyes if that feels safe for you or, if you feel more comfortable with your eyes open, just find a spot on the ground out in front of you and allow your gaze to soften there and your eyes to relax.

3. Begin to slow down your breathing rate, inhaling through the nose for a count of five and exhaling through pursed lips for a count of seven.

4. Repeat, breathing slowly for ten breaths.

5. On your next breath, inhale completely and hold your breath at the top of your inhale.

6. While holding your breath, puff out your cheeks with your lips firmly closed together, so there is nowhere for the air to escape.

7. With puffed cheeks, begin to hum in a high-pitched tone, like you would imagine a bee (note you will naturally begin to exhale through your nose as you are humming).

8. Continue humming with your cheeks puffed until you naturally finish your exhale.

9. Let your cheeks and face relax and breathe normally for
    three breaths.

10. Repeat this sequence ten times.

Music

Music has been deeply intertwined with the human experience for thousands of years and there are many reasons why we are drawn to music as humans.

If you have ever listened to a song that has brought you to tears or felt like you were in a slump only to find yourself singing and moving your body to your favorite tune, then you understand the unique power and impact that music can have on our emotions.

One reason why music can create such an emotive experience is through the connective reaction that occurs within the brain between the melody and memories. Listening to music switches on many parts of the brain involved in memory processing, triggering connections and associations. We actually *feel* the music as an experience within our own bodies.

Furthermore, recent studies have shown that listening to pleasurable music lights up parts of the brain that deal with emotions and rewards, increasing dopamine levels both in the brain and body.

Is it any wonder that music has been enjoyed throughout human history? We are only just scratching the surface on the beautiful dance that occurs between music and human physiology, including how music can support the regulation of our nervous system.

Just like vocal prosody, music can send the same cues of safety via the ear, activating your ventral vagal pathways and vagus nerve. With the right song you can cause your body to experience a physiological response that calms you down. Research shows that listening to slow, sedative and rhythmic music can lead to a decrease in heart rate, blood pressure and breathing rate.

The benefits of music are not only reserved to the songs that you listen to, but also the music that you can make yourself. The voice box is innervated by the vagus nerve, so simply using your voice activates your vagus nerve. Singing and humming are innate human resources that we find ourselves doing without even really thinking about them. When you sing or hum, you also change the pattern of your breath from shallow to deep, as well as extending exhalation. Slow, diaphragmatic breathing, as you now know, is a direct line to activating the vagus nerve and increasing HRV.

Each and every human on this planet is so unique, but it's beautiful to know that music is a resource that connects every one of us to each other. The diversity of our musical taste and abilities is so varied, from techno to classical, but all with the innate capacity to evoke emotion and help to regulate our nervous system.

You are encouraged to welcome music into your life wherever you can—explore genres, artists and bands to find which evoke emotions and sensations, and don't forget your own voice!

Make your own nervous system playlists

Music has a place for every nervous system state, and you can consciously curate reconnective and regulating experiences for yourself depending on which state you recognize you are in.

Your music preferences are unique to you, so make it your own—give the different states of your nervous system a name and then have some fun exploring and creating a playlist that takes you on a journey through that state.

For example:

- **Ventral vagal playlist** could be filled with songs that have that fun energy in them and that you love to sing along to. You may want to sprinkle in a few slower and calming tunes to the playlist too to balance it out.
- **Fight-or-flight playlist** could be those fast-paced, high-tempo songs that make you want to move your body and get any excess energy that is circulating in your nervous system up and out.
- **Dorsal vagal playlist** could be slow, rhythmic and repetitive songs that have a looping effect—over the course of the playlist the tempo and pace of the songs may pick up, increasing the feeling of energy within your body.

Music can help us deepen our sense of connection to ourselves and to others, activating our ventral vagal state and social engagement systems. Music can also take us on a journey through emotions and offer space to release and regulate our nervous systems through the full-body and mind experience that it creates.

If you welcome music into your life, it can teach you to hold space for heavy or sticky emotions and thoughts, as well as create feelings of connection—that you are not alone with your experiences.

HOW TO INTEGRATE THE PRACTICES

Talk about going out with a bang: Phase Three was an absolute powerhouse! I am so proud of you for working your way through the final phase of the Reset Program. This third phase expanded your knowledge and understanding of your vagus nerve—including how to monitor the activity of the vagus nerve via HRV and other ways that you can nurture and strengthen your vagal tone.

The knowledge that you have gained from Phase Three (along with Phases One and Two) are not simple "one and done" practices. Instead, what you have grown into and integrated over these phases is a new paradigm, a new way of being; one that connects the mind and body to create structure and space for you to move through life in a way that feels safe, supported and exciting for you.

In order for your expansion to continue, it's important that you keep practicing and exploring these resources and rituals consistently. Many of the new resources in Phase Three may replace some of those from Phase One or Two—that's the natural progression of phased work.

Just remember that you are in control of your movement between phases and any of the practices that you desire.

This means that depending on the current state of your nervous system and your life circumstances, at any point in time, you can simply shift your practices to match what you need. For example, if you are dealing with a big life transition or a decision that is causing a feeling of uncertainty and lack of safety, returning to be held by the practices of Phase One will allow you to re-establish your sense of safety. It will give you a secure base to anchor to through this season of your life.

In a moment, we will look at how Phase Three practices may integrate into your current daily rituals, but before we do, I want to impress upon you that you do not and should not do everything all at once. Take what you need and trim what is no longer serving you.

The practices that are in bold are Phase Three practices that you will be introducing. Certain practices have been moved under the heading "optional daily practices," and you can decide whether or not you would like to continue or press pause on these practices for a period of time.

Daily practices

- **Heart rate tracker (daily in the morning)**
- **Mindful movement (choose one that you enjoy and practice two to three times per week)**
  - endurance
  - strength
  - balance
- **Somatic stretching (once per week)**

- **Lifestyle practices (choose one to focus on for one to three months)**
  - sleep (resonant breath training)
  - natural light in the morning
  - cold exposure
- **Reconnective practices (choose one to focus on and utilize two to three times per week)**
  - vocal prosody—breath and vocal-toning practice
  - music—playlists for nervous system states
- Daily Mood Record (night)
- Regulating resources (one)
  - proprioceptive
  - cold exposure
  - singing
  - natural light
  - relaxing music
  - hot shower or bath

Optional daily practices

- Containment exercise
- Body exercises
- Gentle movement (choose one—practice every second or third day)
  - swaying
  - rocking
  - swinging
  - restorative yoga
- Balance exercise (choose one—practice every second or third day)

- glute bridges
- crab walk
- balancing on one foot

One-off practice (but revisited intermittently)
- Nourishing your basic needs journal exercise (create action items)
- Mapping your nervous system (write down list of glimmers and keep handy)

Practices for when needed/desired
- Somatic release—shaking
- Progressive body scan
- Worry Record
- Recognizing and sitting with emotions
- Hyperarousal regulating resources (choose one)
  - proprioceptive
  - cold exposure
  - singing
- Hypoarousal (choose one)
  - natural light
  - relaxing music
  - hot shower or bath

You are encouraged to always listen to and honor your personal needs and desires, so remember to take this only as inspiration to create a plan that fits in with your day-to-day life.

You want your rituals to empower and energize you rather than be chores or tasks that weigh you down. Your rituals should hold space for you when you need comfort and safety, but also challenge you slightly so that your nervous system continues to expand, becoming more resilient.

There is no wrong or right when it comes to how much, how often or how long you practice these rituals—there is only what works for you, so let yourself be your own guiding light, influence and authority on your journey and you will always succeed.

FINAL NOTE

As you have moved through the pages of this book, you have made an empowering statement to yourself and others that your experiences—whether challenging or not—are real.

You can acknowledge that these experiences have helped you survive and cope with certain patterns, but they do not define who you are, nor do they hold you back from being all that you know you can be in your life.

As you move forward, you are reminded that you are not alone in your experiences. I hope that you have found parts of yourself within these pages that allow you to feel well supported and understood.

As you have explored your nervous system, and the vagus nerve in particular, you have gained new insights into how your body affects how you respond to the world around you. By tuning in and listening to the wisdom of your body, you gently cultivate a connected, compassionate and attentive relationship with yourself.

The benefits of reconnecting with your body and emotions are not limited to healing traumatic experiences, anxiety and stress. By fully experiencing your body and all it has to offer—its sensual pleasures, its physical pains, its emotional joys and sorrows—you can experience a deeper sense of self-awareness and fulfillment.

Letting go of old, unhelpful beliefs about yourself will allow you to see and greet your true self with fresh eyes. As you do this, you will find that your body responds in kind by becoming more vibrant and resilient.

By healing emotional wounds and reclaiming trust in your body's innate intelligence, you deepen your connection with trusted others, feel empowered rather than afraid of emotions or decisions, gain greater self-awareness and increase acceptance of the parts of yourself that may have been difficult to face. With this new awareness, you will be able to recognize, nurture and shift survival responses that no longer serve you, and in turn gently guide yourself back to your body and safety. The key is to make these changes from a place of love—to truly care about what's best for yourself, your health and happiness.

Carry the momentum you have gained from this book to keep going, continue growing and to stick with the process of self-discovery.

GLOSSARY

autonomic nervous system (ANS)
Nerves responsible for bodily functions that are outside our active control/without conscious thought: heartbeat, blood pressure, breathing, temperature regulation, heart rate variability, sexual arousal, bowel and bladder control, sweat, circulation, digestion and so on. There are two systems within the ANS: the sympathetic, which governs fight-or-flight responses, and the parasympathetic, or "rest and digest." *(See also homeostasis.)*

central nervous system
Your brain, spinal cord and nerves.

containment
The sense of being held and feeling soothed and safe; it can be achieved by various means, including self-holding exercises.

dissociation
Where a person is physically present but experiences a sense of numbness or distance about the events taking place around them.

dorsal vagal
Immobilization; highly implicated in dissociative/dream state.

emotions
Subconscious and instinctive intangible reactions to your internal and external state and events/environment; emotions have a physiological aspect—they create sensation within the body.

exteroception
Perception of the external environment.

fascia
Connective tissue that surrounds and supports muscle, blood vessels and bones throughout the body. According to somatic therapy, our bodies hold pain and trauma in fascia and muscle tension.

feelings	The *conscious* and *cognitive* interpretation of an underlying emotion is called a feeling.
fight-or-flight response	Nervous system is activated and body is primed to move.
freeze response	Nervous system is activated, resulting in body becoming immobilized.
friend or fawn response	When feeling threatened or in danger, looking to others for safety through befriending, flattering and helping. Also known as the "friend," "please," "appease" or "flock" response.
heart rate variability (HRV)	Measurement of the amount of time between your heartbeats. When there is high variability, the person is said to have high (i.e. good) vagal tone.
homeostasis	The ability of an organism to maintain a stable internal environment while adjusting to changes in its external surroundings. Homeostasis is a dynamic process that can change internal conditions as required to survive external challenges.
hyperarousal	A state of hyper-reactivity to external stimuli that manifests in various physical and psychological symptoms (such as elevated heart rate, respiration and alertness).
hypoarousal	A state in which the individual experiences too little arousal. It is often caused by "freezing" during a traumatic event, leading afterwards to symptoms such as numbness and apathy.
interoception	The ability to sense internal signals from your body, such as hunger.
immobilization	The act of limiting movement or being incapable of movement. Also known as dorsal vagal. One of the three systems of polyvagal theory.

mobilization Also known as the sympathetic nervous system. One of the three systems of polyvagal theory.

neuroception A neural process by which we subconsciously read cues of danger or safety from our environment.

parasympathetic nervous system (PNS) Also known as the rest and digest system, the PNS is one of three branches of the autonomic nervous system. This sparks an immobilization response in your brain and body.

polyvagal theory Explains how our autonomic nervous system is related to social behavior and our ability to feel safe and connected in our environment via its three systems: mobilization, social engagement or immobilization. It looks particularly at the role of the vagus nerve in regulating the emotions and social connection.

proprioception The sense that allows us to perceive the location and movement of our limbs. It encompasses a complex array of sensations, including perception of joint position and muscle force, but it can also include things like awareness, e.g. whether or not we've successfully turned on a lamp once we've reached for it in the dark.

social engagement system Innate attraction to feel safe in our environment and with other people. Also known as ventral vagal or parasympathetic. One of the three systems of polyvagal theory.

somatic therapy "Soma" comes from the Ancient Greek word for body. Somatic therapy is an umbrella term for therapeutic modalities that use the body as a tool to understand and heal emotional trauma.

stress response cycle   The body's inbuilt response when the brain and physical body perceive something as threatening. There is a beginning, middle and end; if the cycle is unable to complete, the emotion can remain stuck in the limbic part of the brain and the body may be in a constant state of alert.

sympathetic nervous system (SNS)   This sparks a mobilization response in your brain and body; works with the parasympathetic nervous system (in opposition) to maintain homeostasis (balance) between action and rest.

trauma   Anything that happens to a person too much, too fast or too soon for them to cope with.

vagal tone   Good vagal tone—achieved through things like activating the vagus nerve by way of full-diaphragm, efficient breathing and high heart rate variability—is associated with a well-regulated nervous system and good control of the emotions.

vagus nerve   Largest nerve in the human body; runs from the brain to the abdomen and is responsible for inducing a relaxed state. It is made up of left and right sides as well as a front (ventral) and back (dorsal). The vagus nerve carries a huge number of signals from the digestive system and various organs to the brain and vice versa. It is the main contributor of the parasympathetic nervous system, aka the rest and digest system.

ventral vagal   When we are connected with others who make us feel safe, connected and supported, we are operating in our "ventral vagal" or parasympathetic nervous system. *(See also social engagement system.)*

RESOURCES

To enhance and support your healing journey, I have put together a brief list of resources that may be useful as you continue to explore new practices and ways of thinking about trauma.

These resources include commonly asked questions that may have come up for you as you worked through this book, as well as educational and inspirational books that you may find useful on your continued journey.

Commonly asked questions

I live alone and I'm scared that if I follow the program, I might get overwhelmed or depressed. How will I know if/when to seek professional help?

The program is designed to give you all the tools you need to make positive and sustainable changes; however, it is not a substitute for professional support. If at any point you feel as though you are experiencing a crisis or more than you can handle on your own, please reach out to someone in your support network or a mental health professional immediately. The program will still be there when you are ready.

What do I look for in a holistic therapist?

Throughout this book we have worked through and integrated practices that are accessible to you in the comfort of your own home. However, working with a holistic therapist can provide guidance to help you create a safe space in which you are able to work through your healing process.

Finding the right therapist can be overwhelming and exhausting, but it is worth taking the time to find someone who fits with your personality, belief system and needs. Below are a few suggestions on what to look for when seeking out a therapist:

- You might want to ask the therapist about their professional qualifications and experience working with individuals on similar topics or issues to your own. You may also want to find out if they have much experience working with people who are dealing with trauma, anxiety, stress and PTSD.
- Ask about the type of therapy they use and whether it is based on any specific approach, such as cognitive behavioral therapy (CBT), mindfulness, polyvagal theory or somatics.
- Ask how often they see their clients and what the typical length of treatment is. You might want to look into whether they have a waiting list or if they offer services on evenings or weekends.
- You could also ask about their fees and what those fees cover. Do they offer free initial consultations or trial sessions?

Ultimately, the most important factor when it comes to choosing a therapist is how safe and comfortable you feel with them. There needs to be a sense of understanding and mutual respect within the therapeutic relationship. This is by far the most underrated factor when it comes to choosing a therapist. You should feel relaxed enough to open up about your experiences without feeling judged. If you don't feel at ease with a therapist, then it doesn't matter how many degrees or how much experience they have. You need to feel safe and respected in order for the therapy to work properly.

Above all, it's okay if you don't feel a connection with your therapist. You can always switch if you're not satisfied, and you should never feel pressured to stay with a therapist who doesn't work for you.

In terms of rituals, what does a typical week look like for someone in Phase Three?

Each of the phases in the book is designed in a way to offer options and explorations into yourself, what works best for you and what fits in best with your current day-to-day life. It's essential throughout all of the phases not to expect instant results. It takes time for the body and mind to adjust—so cut yourself some slack if things don't feel perfect right away!

What is most valuable, when engaging in and integrating any of these practices into your life, is to find the natural flow and rhythm of them. What this means is taking a very honest and realistic snapshot of your day to understand when, where and how practices fit best.

For example, if you live in a busy household with children who head off to school each weekday, you may find yourself rushing around first thing in the morning in order to ensure that they are out of the door on time. This may mean that you don't have much time to sit down and practice your resonant breath training (see page 209) before heading off to work yourself. The solution is not to try to force yourself into sitting down for your practices but, rather, find another way to practice resonant breathing throughout your day. It could be taking five minutes at lunchtime, during your commute home from work or even when you get into bed at night.

In order for habits to stick, they have to make sense. If you find yourself thinking, *I don't have time for this!* then it is unlikely that your new habit will become ingrained in your daily routine. Try to find a part of each day when you can set aside small amounts of time to practice and then stick with it.

It's also important to find a balance between the ritual and your day-to-day life. If you overdo one thing, then it may become a chore. If you do not do it enough, then it may not have an impact or make any difference in your daily life. Consistency looks different for everyone, so find where consistency sits for you. It may be in the mornings, before bed or even while you are on the go. Try out different times of day and see what works best.

When you begin to get the hang of it, you may start to notice that one practice flows into another or there might be an alternative path for when you are feeling a bit stuck in one particular area. Don't be afraid to switch things up if your practices are feeling stale or boring. Listen to your intuition instead of forcing something that is no longer working for you.

Another very important reminder is that, if things don't go exactly as you hoped or planned—maybe you miss a day or two or even a week—it does not mean that you are a failure. In fact, it does not mean anything negative about you at all. What matters is that you choose to start again, regardless of how much time has elapsed or how much you have come off track. This is a practice, not a competition; it is a journey to self-discovery and healing. As long as you are willing to start again, then you are on the right path.

There is no right or wrong way to do the phases. Take what feels best for you from each phase and make it your own. Claim ownership of your daily rituals; allow yourself to make mistakes or discover that you dislike something and then change it. This is how you learn to take care of yourself, and this is how you grow.

Educational and inspirational books

There are many books that will support and inspire you on your journey and help your continual growth. I have compiled a list of some of my favorites. Whether you wish to learn more about yourself, expand your mind or just enjoy a good read, these books are sure to please!

- Dana, Deb, *Polyvagal Exercises for Safety and Connection* (W. W. Norton & Company, 2020)
- Demasio, Antonio, *The Feeling of What Happens* (Vintage, 2000)
- Feldenkrais, Moshe, *Awareness Through Movement* (Thorsons, 1991)

- Frankl, Viktor E., *Man's Search For Meaning* (Rider, 2004)
- van der Kolk, Bessel, *The Body Keeps the Score* (Penguin, 2015)
- Levine, Peter A. with Frederick, Ann, *Waking the Tiger* (North Atlantic Books, 1997)
- Menakem, Resmaa, MSW, LICSW, *My Grandmother's Hands* (Central Recovery Press, 2017)
- Porges, Stephen, *The Polyvagal Theory* (W. W. Norton & Company, 2011)
- Seligman, Martin, *Flourish* (Nicholas Brealey Publishing, 2011)

REFERENCES

Preface: My Story: A Roller Coaster of Emotions
"A recent survey found that a staggering 70 percent of adults in the United States have experienced at least one traumatic event during their lifetimes"
National Council for Mental Wellbeing, "How to manage trauma infographic" (Aug. 2022), retrieved from https://www.thenationalcouncil.org/resources/how-to-manage-trauma-2/.

Chapter 2: How the Nervous System Works
"How the brain processes trauma"
Bremner, J. D., "Traumatic stress: Effects on the brain." *Dialogues in Clinical Neuroscience* 8.4 (2006): 445–61.

Chapter 3: Regulating the Nervous System
"Alcohol has the ability to cross the blood–brain barrier"
Mukherjee, S., "Alcoholism and its effects on the central nervous system." *Current Neurovascular Research* 10.3 (2013): 256–62; Pervin, Z. and Stephen, J. M., "Effect of alcohol on the central nervous system to develop neurological disorder: Pathophysiological and lifestyle modulation can be potential therapeutic options for alcohol-induced neurotoxication." *AIMS Neuroscience* 8.3 (2021): 390.

"Dysfunctional breathing patterns"
Vidotto, L. S., et al., "Dysfunctional breathing: What do we know?" *Jornal Brasileiro de Pneumologia* 45 (2019): e20170347; Kaniusas, E., et al., "Non-invasive auricular vagus nerve stimulation as a potential treatment for Covid19-originated acute respiratory distress syndrome." *Frontiers in Physiology* 11 (2020): 890.

"In the groundbreaking SMILES Trial, researchers demonstrated how nutrition has a significant impact on our mood"

Jacka, F. N., et al., "A randomized controlled trial of dietary improvement for adults with major depression (the "SMILES" trial)." *BMC Medicine* 15.23 (2017).

Chapter 4: Tuning Into Your Body

"This connection between the mind and body is beautifully illustrated in a medical trial undertaken by David Spiegel, Director of Stanford University's Psychosocial Research Laboratory, who found that women with breast cancer who participated in group mindfulness therapy lived longer, had less pain and had a higher quality of life"

Spiegel, D., et al., "Effect of psychosocial treatment on survival of patients with metastatic breast cancer." *The Lancet* 2.8668 (1989): 888–91.

"Further research has also determined that stress reduces our body's ability to fight off infection, illness and disease by altering blood cell function"

Littrell, J., "The mind–body connection: Not just a theory anymore." *Social Work in Health Care* 46.4 (2008): 17-37.

"What's more, studies on individuals with anxiety and depression found increased inflammatory markers that reduced the ability of the body to heal wounds"

Raison, C. L., Capuron, L. and Miller, A. H., "Cytokines sing the blues: Inflammation and the pathogenesis of depression." *Trends in Immunology* 27.1 (2006): 24–31.

Chapter 6: Phase One: Securing Your Base

"Interestingly, studies have found that certain types of touch, such as deep touch through cradling the head, can increase HRV (see page 24) and bring the ventral vagal system (see page 18) online"

Edwards, D. J., et al., "The immediate effect of therapeutic touch and deep touch pressure on range of motion, interoceptive accuracy and heart rate variability: A randomized controlled trial with moderation analysis." *Frontiers in Integrative Neuroscience* 12 (2018): 41.

"In holding yourself, you feel a sense of these physical boundaries; you can feel your body; you can feel the energy occurring within its walls"

Ibid.

"Humming requires control over your inhalation and exhalation and can be used as a calming technique"

Gerritsen, R. J. S. and Band, G. P. H., "Breath of life: The respiratory vagal stimulation model of contemplative activity." *Frontiers in Human Neuroscience* 12 (2018): 397; *See also* van der Kolk, B., *The Body Keeps the Score* (Penguin, 2015).

"Glimmers"

Dana, D., *Polyvagal Practices: Anchoring the Self in Safety* (W. W. Norton & Company, 2023).

Chapter 8: Phase Three: Using Your Superpower

"Approximately 33 percent of adults experience loneliness globally—that is over a third of the population that feels as though they do not have access to genuine human connection with other people"

Statista Research department, "Feeling of loneliness among adults 2021, by country" (29 Nov. 2022), retrieved from https://www.statista.com/statistics/1222815/loneliness-among-adults-by-country/.

ACKNOWLEDGMENTS

Ever since I can remember, I dreamed of becoming an author, whisking readers away on incredible adventures. At the tender age of eight, armed with a wild imagination and a trusty pen, I birthed my very first "book." Picture this: a fantastical tale of alien abduction that unfolded into a jaw-dropping revelation—it was all just a dream! Okay, truth be told, it wasn't exactly a literary masterpiece, but hey, we all have to start somewhere, right?

Back then, I couldn't fathom that this humble dream would one day become a reality—I still have to pinch myself sometimes to believe it's true!

Reflecting on the challenging journey of creating this book, I am humbled by the unexpected complexities and emotional rewards it has brought. It has been a symphony of growth and revelation, weaving challenges together into a tapestry that surpasses my wildest dreams.

In this world of words, I feel a deep sense of gratitude and honor as I extend my thanks to those who supported me and contributed to this journey. Their unwavering support and untold stories of collaboration have truly guided and inspired me along the way.

To Damian, my best friend, partner and husband. You are my rock, my cheerleader, my "first reader," my editor and the person who encouraged me to believe in myself. Words cannot express the appreciation I have for you as a human.

To Anne Reilly, who helped me steer the ship when the seas became rocky. You have been an amazing mentor and friend who generously shared your knowledge of writing and editing as well as your time and energy to ensure that this book would be the best possible version of itself. Thank you for helping me find my voice!

To Olivia and Sophie, my publishers, for taking a chance on me as a first-time author and giving me the opportunity to share my story. Thank you for making me feel as comfortable as possible at every step of the process.

To my editors, Anya and Julia, who helped me find all the mistakes I couldn't see. Thanks for helping me polish the rough edges and elevating this book to its fullest potential!

To my parents, Kerry and John, for nurturing my love of reading as a child by sharing your own passion for books with me. Thank you for teaching me to be confident in my ability to succeed at whatever I set out to do. Your love has helped me become who I am today and will continue to shape my future.

And finally, I want to express my heartfelt gratitude and deep admiration to you, dear reader. Your unwavering courage and innate desire to heal and explore the depths of your inner world have been a constant source of inspiration for me. Your willingness to embark on this transformative journey, to delve into the complexities of human existence and face the challenges it brings is truly remarkable. Through your engagement and open-heartedness, storytelling fulfills its true purpose, providing solace, enlightenment and the opportunity for personal growth. It has been an honor to share this adventure with you, and I wholeheartedly celebrate your unwavering spirit in the pursuit of self-discovery.

INDEX

Note: page numbers in **bold** refer to diagrams.

ABOUT THE AUTHOR

Anna Ferguson is a leading Australian mental health expert and anxiety therapist. She has built an engaged community of 250,000 followers on Instagram, sharing practical, holistic mind-body tools and breaking down barriers and stigma around mental health. Through her work as a counselor, speaker, and author, she provides valuable resources for those who struggle with anxiety, and is striving to change the conversation around mental health. You can visit her online at annatheanxietycoach.com or on Instagram @annatheanxietycoach.

Hi there,

We hope *The Vagus Nerve Reset* helped you. If you have any questions or concerns about your book, or have received a damaged copy, please contact customerservice@penguinrandomhouse.com. We're here and happy to help.

Also, please consider writing a review on your favorite retailer's website to let others know what you thought of the book.

Sincerely,
The Zeitgeist Team